From Death to Birth

Understanding Karma and Reincarnation

Also by Pandit Rajmani Tigunait

Swami Rama of the Himalayas: His Life and Mission

Shakti: The Power in Tantra (A Scholarly Approach)

The Power of Mantra and the Mystery of Initiation

Inner Quest: The Path of Spiritual Unfoldment

Shakti Sadhana: Steps to Samadhi
*   (A Translation of the Tripura Rahasya)*

Yoga on War and Peace

The Tradition of the Himalayan Masters

Seven Systems of Indian Philosophy

Tantra Unveiled: Seducing the Forces of Matter and Spirit

Videos

In the Footsteps of the Sages

Tantric Traditions and Techniques

The Secret of Tantric Rituals

Forbidden Tantra

Tantra and Kundalini

Sri Chakra: The Highest Tantric Practice

Sri Vidya: The Embodiment of Tantra

FROM DEATH TO BIRTH

UNDERSTANDING KARMA AND REINCARNATION

By
Pandit Rajmani Tigunait, Ph.D.

The Himalayan Institute Press
Honesdale, Pennsylvania

The Himalayan Institute Press
RR 1, Box 405
Honesdale, PA 18431

Cover design by Robert Aulicino

The paper used in this publication meets the minimum
requirements of the American National Standard for
Information Sciences—Permanence of Paper for Printed
Library Materials, ANSI Z39.48-1984.

ISBN 0-89389-147-9

To my gurudeva, Sri Swami Rama,
who stands as a beacon on both shores of life

CONTENTS

Introduction

"THE MYSTERY OF LIFE lies in the knowledge of death." These words still resound in my ears. Before I heard them spoken by my gurudeva, Sri Swami Rama, another great yogi had whispered them to me silently, but due to my ignorance I had not heard them.

In October of 1979 I was preparing to fly to the United States for the first time. The day before my departure, I heard that a tantric master known as Datia Wale Swamiji was undergoing dialysis at the All-India Medical Institute in New Delhi. During his stay there the part of the hospital wing where he was housed became a shrine, as this great man was regarded as the blessed son of the Divine Mother. On the days he was not scheduled for dialysis, hundreds of people stood in line to see him. Not wanting to miss this rare opportunity, I went to the hospital and joined the line—but just as I was about to reach his room, visiting hours ended. Deeply disappointed, I turned away.

The next day was his dialysis day and no visitors would be allowed. Nevertheless, before going to the airport, I made one more attempt. My thought was that even if I couldn't see him, I would pay my respects to the building where he was staying. It was late afternoon and dozens of people just like me were standing around without any real expectation of being allowed to see him. But to our surprise, the message came that the tantric master would see us.

He was sitting on a big couch in his room. People would stop at the door, gaze at him for a few seconds and move on, making way for the next person. When my turn came, I looked into the room and immediately bowed my head with respect and bewilderment. He looked so vibrant and healthy it was difficult to believe he was suffering from kidney failure. As I lingered in the doorway to be in his presence for a few extra seconds, he asked, "Whose son are you?"

Knowing he was really asking whose student I was, I replied, "I am a *shishya* [student] of Bhole Baba" [an appellation of Swami Rama's].

Upon hearing Swamiji's name, he burst out joyfully, "Come near me, my son. Where is my brother?" I approached him, and placing my head near his knees told him that these days Swamiji lived in the United States. He began talking about Swamiji in such a loud, energetic voice that his doctors and attendants asked him to be quiet, fearing that he might collapse from the exertion. He roared with laughter. Looking at me, he demanded, "Tell these people what the source of life is." When I remained quiet, he answered his own question. "*Shakti,* the eternal and all-pervading divine force, intrinsic to the Almighty Being, is the source of life. She is the Divine Mother. Go, my son. May the grace of the Divine Mother be showered on you. And tell my brother we will meet again on the other shore."

I paid my homage and departed. The swami was a big man, but his skin hung in folds—it looked like he had lost more than a hundred pounds—yet he was radiant. I was overwhelmed by his vibrancy and apparent good health. He must have been in his nineties, but it seemed that old age was too timid to show her face to him. Still, he was dying. Even more puzzling, he was joyful in the face of death. He appeared to be eagerly waiting to embrace something more precious and delightful than the world he would leave behind, something that would come after death. Later I heard that he died shortly after I saw him.

That same night I flew to the States. I had no opportunity to share my thoughts and feelings about this encounter with anyone until the summer of 1980 when I was with my gurudeva. After I told Swamiji about this incident, I asked him bluntly, "What was he so happy about? How can a person be free from fear and anxiety when he clearly hears death knocking at the door?"

Swamiji replied, "He had no fear of death because he knew where he was going. He was happy because the loss of worldly objects had no meaning for him. Adepts don't die—they cast off their body at will. Even the shadow of death cannot touch them; they are immortal. They have unveiled the mystery of death long before the actual moment of death arrives. They understand that death is simply a habit of the body—a change which to an ignorant person appears to be a big loss.

"To this tantric adept," Swamiji continued, "both shores of life were fully known, so he was free from anxiety. He was happy here and will continue to be happy hereafter. Those lacking this knowledge cling to life. Afraid of the unknown, they do not want to move on to the stage of life which follows death. For ignorant people death is like an eviction. It is accompanied by pain. Not knowing how to cope with this, they close their eyes, become unconscious, and die with no awareness of the process of dying. Adepts die with full awareness, and that is why they walk with certainty and security toward their destination."

In the long process of learning from Swamiji and other adepts, and through contemplation on the scriptures such as the Upanishads, the Puranas, and tantric texts, I have come to see that death is the greatest of all teachers, provided that we remain awake when the lesson is being imparted. The journey of the soul from birth to death is quite straightforward. We are born; we grow; and with varying degrees of pleasure and pain, comfort and discomfort, we become adults; we strive to survive and procreate; we grow old and die. This journey is automatic and leads nowhere but to death, decay, and destruction. If we do not come to understand what lies between death and birth while we are alive, we get sucked into the infinite domain of anxiety and uncertainty. Clouds of insecurity, fear, and grief begin to hover around us long before death approaches. We make every effort to make ourselves secure by hoarding worldly objects and by harboring religious beliefs, yet we know that life is bound to be consumed by death. No matter how desperately we try to ignore this fact, we have to face it eventually, even if only at the last moment of our life.

The scriptures claim that the state of consciousness at the time of death by and large determines the state of consciousness in the afterlife. Individual consciousness returns on the same train of thought by which it departed. If we die unconsciously, we have no conscious control over our thought patterns, but instead we are trapped by a powerful wave of thought emerging from long-cherished emotions, which serve as the wellsprings of our thoughts. They stem from the repeated experiences of our actions throughout our life.

Whenever we perform an action we are bound to reap its fruits, which are either pleasant or unpleasant. We either cling to these fruits or attempt to get rid of them, and in the process, we again perform actions. These actions in turn breed fruits, and these fruits breed more actions. Life between birth and death is a field of karma in which we sow and reap and sow again.

If we do not extricate ourselves from this cycle we are one day harvested by the force of time. Then we are no longer the creator of our karmas, but instead are created by them. This is what the scriptures refer to as the bondage of karma. Freedom lies in breaking this cycle, for only then are we able to unveil the mystery that lies in the realm between death and birth. Only then do we truly become the creator of our own destiny.

The scriptures have promised (and the adepts have demonstrated) that those who are free from karma can leave their body consciously before death draws near. And while mastering the process of casting off the body voluntarily and consciously, the adepts go all the way to death, and return again and again. For an ordinary person death is accompanied by darkness; for "seekers of death" it is filled with light. In that light, these adepts study the interior of their own mind. Their experience bears no resemblance to the near-death experiences reported by those who fall into the jaws of death and somehow escape, and their story of heaven and hell, purgatory and limbo, God, the devil, and angels is different from what we learn from religious texts, and more meaningful.

For the rest of us, the journey of the soul from death to birth is determined mainly by our karmas—the actions we perform in the interval between birth and death. That is why the key to

unveiling the mystery of rebirth and reincarnation is understanding karma and its effect on our mind and consciousness.
This understanding in turn brightens our knowledge of how
we can eventually become the creators of our destiny rather
than its product. As we shall see in the following pages, discovering the dynamics of karma, its role in the formation of
our destiny, and its effect on the process of dying not only
sheds light on the multi-layered mystery concealed behind the
curtains of heaven and hell, it also determines whether the soul
comes back to this world along the muddy path of rebirth,
returns along the high road of reincarnation, or descends
through divine birth.

CHAPTER ONE

LIVING EXPERIENCES OF THE DYNAMICS OF KARMA

WE LOOK AT THE WORLD around us and see pockets of incredible suffering, and wonder why. Some people are visited by disease, starvation, and violence, while others go through life unscathed. We see people involved in all kinds of unhealthy, unethical, and harmful activities who appear to prosper, while some who are honest, hardworking, and well intentioned encounter only failure. And we read accounts of people who were so spiritually evolved that they were capable of healing others and transforming their lives, yet who suffered from painful and fatal diseases themselves. Why?

According to yoga the answers to these questions lie in the knowledge of individual and collective karmas—knowledge that explains the mystery of birth and death and all that lies between. As a student I took up the study of philosophy because I was intent on understanding the root cause of fortune and misfortune. Yet for all my reading and pondering, the answers eluded me. I began to grasp the theory of karma as expounded in the scriptures only after spending time with a number of highly accomplished yogis. During my time with them, these spiritual adepts unveiled some of the subtle mysteries that lie in the realm beyond intellectual explanations.

One of my early teachers was Swami Sadanand. I was fortunate enough to meet him when I was a student of Sanskrit at the University of Allahabad. This gentle saint lived on a bank of the Ganges on the outskirts of the city. He was well versed in the scriptures as well as the secular sciences. In the years before I met my gurudeva, Sri Swami Rama, he was one of those from whom I sought knowledge of *Sri Vidya*, the most exalted of spiritual sciences. Swami Sadanand did not promise to teach me that science, but he guided me to the scriptures related to Sri Vidya practice, and explained that learning and practicing Sri Vidya requires good karmas as well as God's grace. He told me that both could be gathered by practicing the *gayatri* mantra, adding that this mantra can erase negative karmas, create new positive karmas, and open the channel for God's grace.

Although neither these instructions nor the theories he expounded from the scriptures really made sense to me at the time, Swami Sadanand's love, compassion, and kindness, as well as his knowledge of the scriptures, infused my heart with deep devotion and faith in him. On several occasions he explained the law of karma, yet it remained abstract and incomprehensible to me until I began to get a glimpse of its operation in my own life and the lives of some of those around me.

Answers and More Questions

Swami Sadanand was kind to everyone and gave medicines freely to the sick, yet when I was sick he paid no attention. I could not understand this. Then one day I received the news that my mother, who lived in a distant village, had been having terrible headaches for more than a month and had recently lost her eyesight. In a panic I went to the saint and begged him to give me medicine for her. He said, "Medicines are too weak to change the course of karma. I will give you medicine for your mother if you want, but it is better that you do the recitation of *aditya hridayam*" [a prayer to the sun revealed to the sage Agastya].

I was puzzled, but I remained in Allahabad, sixty miles from my mother's village, and did twelve recitations of this prayer every day while continuing my routine at the university. Eventually my sister told me that my mother had suddenly gotten well. Deeply grateful—and curious about the relationship between this prayer and my mother's recovery—I went to Swami Sadanand. "How can prayer or mantra practice help not only the practitioner but also someone at a distance?" I asked.

With a smile he replied, "Intense *tapas, samadhi* [spiritual absorption], mantra *sadhana*, the grace of God, selfless service, and *satsanga* [the company of saints] create a powerful positive karma in a short period of time. And this can neutralize the effect of previous negative karmas." He got up and pulled out the *Yoga Sutra* with the commentary of Vyasa and showed me the exact passage he was quoting.

When he put the law of karma into this context, I began to understand the *Yoga Sutra* and other scriptures more profoundly than before, but I was still unable to really grasp the dynamics of karma and reincarnation. Then one Sunday morning I came to the ashram quite early and found Swami Sadanand in the company of a gentleman who suffered from epileptic fits so violent and frequent that someone always accompanied him to make sure he didn't hurt himself. The saint gave him something that looked like ash.

"Take this medicine every morning," he instructed, "but only after you have fed grain to the wild birds. After your morning ablutions, get some barley, cracked wheat, and other grains, invite the birds to come to you, and feed them. Once they have eaten, take this medicine. Only then may you take your meal."

When the man left, I said, "Sir, I understand the value of taking medicine. But why does he have to feed the birds?"

Swami Sadanand replied, "You should watch. When he is cured, I will explain."

For three days the poor fellow starved because the birds would not eat the grain he scattered for them. Then, on the fourth day, they accepted his offering and he started taking the medicine. It became his routine to feed the birds before starting his day. In a month his fits came less frequently; within six months he was cured.

When I asked Swami Sadanand to explain, he said, "Birds are part of nature. Their relationship with humans is not contaminated by selfishness and expectations. They are happy when you serve them, but they do not mind if you don't. They operate on instinct alone—they make no personal choices and have no agendas. Serving them is serving nature, which is the repository of all our karmas.

"Our individual *chitta* [the unconscious mind] and *karmashaya* [the vehicle of our karmas] always work in conformity with nature, *prakriti,* which encompasses not only plants, rivers, and the rest of the natural environment—it also encompasses the primordial energy-field which is the source of and locus for this material world. By sacrificing your comforts and giving away that which you believe to be yours, you pay off your karmic debts in the subtle realm. And it is these karmic debts that are the cause of your present misery."

This explanation, brief as it was, gave me enough material for several years of study and contemplation. But the more I studied and pondered the mystery of karma, the more questions came into my mind: Can we pay off our karmic debts only by feeding other creatures? Aren't humans a part of nature too? Is it possible to pay off our karmic debts even though we don't know what they are? Does the karma of one life affect our future lives? If so, how?

My mother's recovery and the cure of the epileptic suggested that there is a way of getting around the law of karma, but the questions remained: Do we attain freedom from the bondage of karma only after paying off all our karmic debts? Or can we get exemptions by practicing intense tapas, attaining samadhi, undertaking mantra sadhana, performing selfless service, being in the company of saints and sages, and obtaining the grace of God? Is obtaining God's grace like declaring bankruptcy—because the burden of our karmic debts is too great to offset by other means?

Hoping to find answers to these questions, I switched my studies from Sanskrit literature and Ayurveda so I could concentrate on the scriptures and philosophical texts. In addition to spending time with Swami Sadanand, I began to visit dozens of the swamis who came to the annual spiritual festival on the banks of the Ganges in Allahabad. Many of these learned teachers answered some of my questions, but often their answers were too profound for me to fully comprehend. I found that the verbal answers I got were usually less helpful than the understanding I gained by observing the spontaneous actions of these saints.

For example, one of these holy men was visited by a healthy young man who, for no apparent reason, had become obsessed with the thought that he would soon meet with a fatal accident. After listening to his problem, the saint instructed the young man to stay with him at his temporary ashram on the riverbank for a while.

After a few days the young man became impatient. Early one morning he decided to take the next train to his home in the town of Jhariya. The saint strongly advised him not to go, but the young man argued that he needed to get back to his job. So the saint said that he himself was ill, that he needed medicine from town that only the young man could get for him. He soothed the young man's impatience by assuring him he could leave the next day or even by the evening train that same day, but because his own illness and advanced age made it uncertain that they would ever meet again, it was important that the young man do him this one final service.

The young man agreed. He went to town and got the medicine, and missed the morning train to Jhariya. The next day brought the news: the train had wrecked, killing more than one hundred passengers and injuring several hundred more. The young man, overwhelmed with gratitude, now wanted to stay and serve the saint, but the holy man insisted that he go home.

After observing this and similar incidents, I realized the truth of the scriptural statement that one means of counteracting negative karmas is to be in the company and the service of saints. Yet I still could not understand why serving holy women and men in the here-and-now can erase the effect of karma created in the past. I was curious to know who maintains such a precise record of karmas, and further, why some have the wisdom to know the karmic records and others don't. I also wondered why some yoga masters, who evidently understand the cause of other people's problems and help them skillfully, remain indifferent toward helping themselves.

Questions continued to haunt my mind: Is it easier to know someone else's problems than it is to know our own? Is it easier to help others than to help ourselves? Are these wise people bound by certain spiritual laws? Is that why, in spite of having the capacity to know and remove the cause of their problems, they don't do it?

As time passed I found some answers, but still my list of questions grew. Then one day I gained direct experience of a particular spiritual practice, and this changed the course of my own destiny.

It was the winter of 1982. My gurudeva, Sri Swami Rama, was staying in New Delhi and I was with him, preparing to depart for the United States that evening. Suddenly he asked me, "So when are you going?" I told him the time. A little later he asked again, "So when are you going?" I gave the same answer. Later he asked yet again, adding, "Do you have to go?" I explained that I had classes to teach and should get back, but he didn't seem to be listening. This dialogue was repeated again and again during the next several hours. Finally I realized he didn't want me to go, although I had no idea why. I called the airline and canceled my flight. A short time later he asked again, "Are you going?"

When I said, "No," he said, "Good. You should go to Rishikesh and do such-and-such practice while you stay at the ashram. Every day visit the Virbhadra temple."

So I went to Rishikesh and did the practice. On the last day

I began to feel extremely sluggish. Every time I picked up my mala beads and started to repeat the mantra, I fell asleep. I got up and washed my face with cold water several times, but couldn't stay awake. Finally, while sitting in my meditative pose I nodded off. The mala dropped from my hand and I began to dream a dream so vivid that I knew it was real.

In this dream I saw myself being driven along the familiar route from New York City to Swamiji's headquarters in Pennsylvania, where I live. The driver, a woman I will call Laura, often drove me to New York. She was driving along happily as usual when a car suddenly entered the freeway from the exit ramp and headed toward us. It was coming directly at us. If Laura braked abruptly, the car behind us would crash into us. If we swerved onto the shoulder or into the other lane, we would collide with the cars around us. There was no time and no option: a head-on collision was inevitable. Then, a fraction of a second before the crash, an extraordinarily tall man clad in white appeared between the two cars and prevented the collision. He picked us up—me in one hand and Laura in the other—and deposited us on the median strip.

I woke up to find my mala on the floor. My entire being was suffused with a powerful mixture of fear and joy—fear from the near collision, and joy from the loving touch of the being who had plucked me out of harm's way. There were goose bumps all over my body. But I still had lots of japa to do before the practice was finished, so I put the experience out of my mind and concentrated on the mantra.

Shortly afterwards I returned to the United States and resumed my normal routine. As time passed I forgot about the dream.

That spring Laura drove me to New York City to teach a

class. On our way home she suddenly announced that her heart was pounding and she was afraid to drive any further. She said that for the past several days she had been seeing a head-on collision in her mind's eye. Not wishing to refuse to drive me to New York, she had tried to dismiss her fear. But now it had become overwhelming—she was too frightened to drive much further.

As she told me this, I remembered my dream and saw that we were approaching the spot where it had taken place. I also remembered Swamiji saying that whatever happens in the external world has already happened long before in the inner world. Suddenly I understood that this incident had already taken place; the mysterious being in white had already saved us, so there was no need to fear. But I could not say such things to Laura.

The exit ramp that the car had come down in my dream was just ahead. I tried to distract Laura by engaging her in conversation, but she was becoming more and more agitated. We were in the right lane, approaching the exit ramp, when a car suddenly came down it heading directly for our car. As Laura began to brake, the cars behind and beside us braked and swerved, but a collision seemed inevitable. In that instant the question flashed through my mind: Should I take off my seat belt so that the white-clad being could get me out of the car more easily? Almost simultaneously another thought came: What difference does it make? A physical being can't help, and for a subtle force a seat belt is nothing. So I closed my eyes and braced myself. Just as we were about to crash I saw the white-clad being appear between the two cars, pluck Laura and me out of our car, and deposit us on the right shoulder of the road.

I opened my eyes and found myself standing next to Laura, my body infused with the same mixture of fear and delight I had experienced after the dream in Rishikesh. Again, I had goose bumps all over my body. Our car was standing almost nose-to-nose with the oncoming car, and our front doors were wide open. Some of the cars behind us had collided, although none seriously. Drivers were leaning out of their windows shouting. I asked Laura if she was all right. She smiled and said, "I'm fine." So while the drivers around us were yelling and writing down each other's license numbers, we got into our car and drove away.

For several weeks I wondered about the tall being clad in white. Who or what was it? According to the Christian faith he would be an angel; from the Indian perspective he would be an immortal sage or yogi. I had no idea what it was. I had no sense that I had known or experienced it before—except in the dream. So why did it protect me? Was it the personified form of the mantra Swamiji had given me to practice in Rishikesh? Was he the same sage that had protected Swamiji when he fell while lost in the mountains? I had no particular feelings of love for that being. But I did feel an overwhelming sense of gratitude toward Swamiji. Had he himself helped me by assuming that form? Or had that being appeared at his request?

My mind kept returning to the practice I had done in Rishikesh. Yet I doubted that this experience was due solely to that, because I knew many people who had repeated the same mantra hundreds of times without any significant change in their circumstances. Had Swamiji used this practice to evoke a force of protection powerful enough to prevent me from reaping the fruit of my past karma?

What happened to Laura after this incident raised even more questions. For a couple of weeks she seemed to be in another, more blissful, world. Her heart was brimming with joy and with gratitude toward Swamiji and the spiritual tradition he represented. But within three weeks her mood changed. Although she had been a student of Swamiji's for a long time and was close to my family, she now kept her distance from us, and became indifferent and then hostile toward Swamiji. In the fourth week, she left the Institute. She had many complaints, but the main one was that Swamiji was selfish. She said she was disappointed that Swamiji did not want others to live a happy life.

I found this incomprehensible. I wanted Swamiji to explain, but I knew if I asked him what had happened he would simply remain silent. But one day, while I was still puzzling over these events, I came across a passage in one of the Puranas that answered my question. In the course of a lengthy story, this scripture made it clear that no one can interfere with the law of karma. All the forces, seen or unseen, that function in this mortal world are governed by this law. Birth and death and all that happens between these two events are dependent on the law of karma. The law of karma determines the situation into which we are born in this lifetime, and into which we will be born in the next. But there is one way that karmic events can be amended. The law of divine providence—which is the inherent power of God—is beyond the law of karma and can amend karmic events—although it rarely does so. Nothing is impossible in the realm of divine providence. What is more, we can connect with the divine will through intense tapas, mantra sadhana, samadhi, devotion to God, the company of saints, and selfless service. When that happens, the reshaping of karmic events begins to take place by itself. The scripture also stated that receiving the grace of the divine will requires preparation, and that even greater preparation is needed in order to retain and assimilate this grace once it has been received. Faith in God and surrender to God's will make this possible, and this attitude of faith and surrender is created through meditation, prayer, japa, contemplation, self-study, and service to those whose minds and hearts are totally filled with God-consciousness.

When I put Laura's behavior into the context of this message, I got the answer to my question. It was possible that in my case the force of karma had not interfered with the divine will because that japa practice of eleven days in Rishikesh had given me the opportunity to assimilate the grace flowing through the practice. But Laura had not had a similar opportunity, and that may have been why her initial joy was soon undermined by doubt and fear.

Who Are We?

I had heard Swamiji expound on different aspects of yoga, meditation, and spirituality since 1976. One of his constant, underlying messages was that we humans are the makers of our own destiny; through thinking, we become what we want to be. Even though generally the law of karma cannot be avoided, Swamiji also said repeatedly that if we cultivate *sankalpa shakti* (the power of will and determination), we can reshape some of those karmas which have not yet started to manifest in present events.

Yet neither Swamiji nor the scriptures tell us clearly how to know what our karmas are or when it is appropriate to make an effort to modify them. The scriptures offer hundreds of prescriptions for working with our karmas to minimize their negative effects, but they also warn teachers not to pass on such instructions unless their students are fully prepared. The problem is that the preparation is quite arduous—we must commit ourselves to demanding practices when we are still caught in karmic whirlpools. At the same time that we are undertaking spiritual practices aimed at erasing our negative karmas, we must struggle with a host of obstacles—obstacles which, according to the scriptures, are also due to the karmas we have already accumulated. So where do we start, and how?

The scriptures tell us that our karma impels us to float along the current of time. During this journey we pass countless islands—other individual souls who are also impelled by karma. While we are together we become attached to each other, spend a little time together, then part. Due to our attachment we try to linger, but our karma carries us onward. This journey is not always smooth. In places, the impetus of our karma has created whirlpools of varying strengths and sizes, and when we pass through them in the journey of life we experience turmoil—pleasure, pain, loss, gain, honor, insult, and all the rest. Once caught in karmic whirlpools, we swirl around and around and reach nowhere. This is the cycle of birth and death—being born, struggling for survival, eventually being defeated by death, and being born again. It leads us nowhere.

The sages have drawn maps and created a system of navigation to enable us to extricate ourselves from the current and reach the other shore of life, a realm free from karmic impetus. Spirituality is the process of learning to extricate ourselves from these whirlpools and cross the river without being caught again, and spiritual practice involves obtaining a map and learning to navigate the river of time. The reward is *moksha:* freedom from the bondage of karma.

The map is complex. Gaining the skill to read it entails studying the dynamics of karma and learning how we create karmas for ourselves, how we get entangled in them, and how we can disentangle ourselves. We must discover which karmas can be avoided and which cannot. Once armed with this knowledge, we will no longer waste time struggling with karmas that cannot be avoided. Instead we can recognize the pattern of the whirlpool and learn to extricate ourselves at the first opportunity, rather than swirling round and round endlessly. Reading the karmic map also entails discovering that we have the freedom to choose whether or not to enter certain karmic whirlpools. Once we know this, we can cross the river of time without getting caught.

The map laid out in the scriptures tells us that there are three distinct karmic streams: *sanchita* (dormant) karmas, *prarabdha* (active) karmas, and *kriyamana* (potential) karmas. We have the freedom to choose whether or not to entangle ourselves in dormant and potential karmas, but in the case of the active karmas we have almost no choice. That is why it is known as destiny—prarabdha karma is almost impossible to alter. Even those who operate at the level of divine providence and have the power to go beyond the law of karma must not interfere with destiny.

Dormant and potential karmas are just as important as the karma that constitutes destiny, but prarabdha karma draws our attention because the life we are now living—the circumstances surrounding us—is the direct result of this karma. We are already in its grip. And if this prarabdha karma—destiny—cannot be amended, then in what sense are we the

makers of our own destiny? In most cases we experience ourselves as victims of destiny, not as its creator. Are we shaped by
our destiny, or are we the shapers of our destiny? Is destiny our
creator, or are we the creators of destiny? Who are we?

The answers to these questions lie in discovering how karmas are created in the first place. But before we launch into
this inquiry, let us examine the relationship among dormant,
active, and potential karmas and gain some understanding of
the interaction among them and how they become predomi-
nant in different phases of our lives.

CHAPTER TWO

DORMANT, ACTIVE, AND POTENTIAL KARMAS

THE WORD *KARMA* means "action." All of our actions are karmas except the ones we are in the process of performing. These are *kriyas;* completed actions are karmas. The seeds of karma lie in the kriya, because our present actions instantly turn into completed actions. When an action is completed, the action itself no longer exists in its gross form, but the result of that action manifests sooner or later. Both the action and its result are stored in their subtle forms in the unconscious mind and are known as "karmas."

These days the word *karma* has taken on negative connotations. People in the East as well as the West make statements such as "My karma caught up with me" when something unpleasant happens. This is a distortion of the concept. Karma can be positive or negative, uplifting or degrading. The law of karma is simply "As you sow, so shall you reap."

All cultures share the belief that if we do good we will reap good results. The concept of good differs from place to place and from time to time, but the conviction that there is a causal relationship between good actions and good results and bad or wrong actions and bad results is fundamental to all societies. And regardless of what the highest goal of life is thought to be, spiritually uplifting actions are universally seen as the means of purifying the way of the soul, just as base actions are seen as contaminating.

Any action we perform—whether mental, verbal, or physical—creates a subtle impression in our unconscious mind. When we continually repeat the same action these impressions are strengthened, until eventually they become so powerful that, unable to resist their strong currents, we are swept into performing actions that match these impressions. In other words, subtle impressions *(samskaras)* are born from our actions, and, in turn, our actions are motivated by subtle impressions. This is a vicious cycle that, once in motion, is difficult to break. This cycle—actions creating impressions, which in turn drive our actions—is the law of karma.

We do not know when this process began, so we call it "beginningless." According to the yogis, until we gain access to that realm of consciousness where the subtle impressions are formed and all our previous deeds are stored, it is fruitless to brood about how and why we performed our first action, created a corresponding subtle impression, and thus got caught in the cycle. What is useful is knowing how to free ourselves. From a practical standpoint, the first step is to discover how to burn or erase negative karmas and engender positive ones.

As we discussed in chapter one, the yogis categorize all karmas into three main divisions: *sanchita* (dormant), *prarabdha* (active), and *kriyamana* (potential) karmas. The literal meaning of *sanchita karma* is "stored karma." These are dormant;

they will become active only when conditions are ripe. Like seed corn stored in a silo, sanchita karmas will sprout and bear fruit if they are planted in a viable place in the proper season and receive the right amount of sustenance.

Prarabdha karmas have already started producing fruit. These are like seed corn which has been removed from the silo, planted, and is now growing. The life of these plants is determined by the fertility of the soil, climatic conditions, and the prevalence of disease and insects. Corn plants growing in a field have no choice but to withstand whatever conditions they encounter and to strive to produce ears of corn. Once a plant has sprouted there is no way that it can return to its seed form to await more favorable growing conditions. Our active karmas are like these plants

When conditions are favorable our dormant karmas become active, shaping our life and its circumstances. Like sprouting corn, once we begin our outward journey we are totally dependent on what life has to offer. Just as a farmer tends the plants, hoping for a good harvest (although he knows that much of the plant's fate is not in his hands), we try to do what is best for ourselves and those we love. Our success depends on many variables, most of which are unpredictable.

Prarabdha karmas constitute our destiny. (*Prarabdha* literally means "already in the process of producing fruits.") There is not much to be done once the cycle of karma has reached the stage of destiny, but the process of reaping the fruits of destiny can be managed wisely. When our active karmas have run their course, for example, their fruits can be stored or given up. If we are attached to the fruits of our actions we will store them, and if we do, there is a good chance they will sprout and the cycle will begin again.

Potential karmas are those which have not yet been created. The literal translation of *kriyamana karma* is "karma yet to be performed." These can be compared to the ears of corn which have not yet formed. If we let the plant grow, it will form ears and eventually yield fully mature kernels in the natural course of events. Similarly, under the so-called normal circumstances of life—the conditions into which we are born and under which we live—we find ourselves performing actions, all of which bear fruit.

Here the analogy breaks down. Corn has no free will but depends totally on nature for its survival. We seem to have more free will and are less dependent on nature. We may not be able to stop the course of events caused by prarabdha karma, but we are free either to accumulate the fruits of our karmas or to renounce them. Hoarding the fruits creates an environment of further involvement—potential karmas—but those who entertain destiny joyfully and wisely, who are free from both attachment and aversion to the experiences that destiny brings, renounce the fruit of their actions and thus do not form potential karmas.

Yoga texts use another metaphor, one drawn from archery, to explain the three types of karmas. (At the time these texts were compiled, archery was not a sport but an essential skill for a warrior.) Sanchita (dormant) karmas are like arrows stored in the quiver, ready to be fit into the bow. Prarabdha (active) karmas are like arrows already in flight. Kriyamana (potential) karmas are like arrows that have not yet been made, although all the components are present. Arrows, like any other weapon, are made for a reason. The same reason that impels us to make or purchase arrows impels us to use them. Once they have been shot, the warrior requires more arrows, so more will be made. They will be stored in the warrior's quiver, shot in due course, and new arrows will be produced and placed in the quiver. The cycle of karmas—from dormant, to active, to potential, back to dormant, and so on—continues in the same fashion.

History tells us that there has never been a weapon manufactured that was not eventually used; similarly, once karmas have been created and stored, they must show their effect somewhere, sometime. With weapons, the safest course is to destroy them before the impulse to use them arises. If this is not possible, the next best option is to entrust them to someone who is wise and balanced. This also applies to dormant karmas—the safest course is to either burn them in the fire of knowledge or surrender them to the Divine.

This is possible only if we have been able to conduct a thorough inventory of our karmic deeds. But most of us have neither the knowledge nor the ability to enter the basement of our unconscious mind, where our karmic deeds are stored in the form of subtle impressions. Some of us do not even want to know about our karmic deeds because we do not want to be called to account by our own conscience. Yet if we remain oblivious to the unmanifest causes of our present problems we have no way of either eradicating them or preventing other problems in the future. Not knowing the causes of disease may help us stay free from worry, but it will not prevent us from contracting a disease if we are exposed to its causes. Similarly, ignorance regarding our dormant karmas may give us the illusion that everything is fine, but this illusion will be shattered when our dormant karmas manifest and become active, taking the form of destiny.

Dormant Karma (Sanchita)

In the process of self-discovery, the process that allows us to navigate the karmic whirlpools safely, we must penetrate the layer of our being where our karmas are deposited. When we know what they are and how numerous they are, we can make the decision whether to throw them into the fire of knowledge, thereby disidentifying ourselves from them, or to surrender them to the Divine. The following story sheds some light on the yogic method of reaching the realm of dormant karmas and attaining freedom from them.

———

Long ago there lived a yogi named Jaigishavya who undertook a long uninterrupted practice of intense *tapas* (austerities) before attaining enlightenment. Aided by the indomitable power of his will, he defied hunger, thirst, sleep, and fatigue. Even though his body became emaciated, his senses and mind turned inward and his consciousness rose upward.

Eventually the concentrated force of his consciousness penetrated the realm of existence where the ordinary mind cannot reach. Then, as recounted in the scriptures, he transcended his body-consciousness and saw the relationship between the body, the senses, and the different faculties of mind. As his practice intensified, his awareness became so concentrated that he gained direct experience of the contents of his mind, ego, and intellect. Finally he entered the vast realm of the unconscious mind, known as *chitta,* where he encountered the dormant karmas related to his millions and millions of past lives. But in this state of deep spiritual absorption, he became disoriented. Although his mind was clear and one-pointed, he could not tell whether he was dreaming or whether the contents of his unconscious mind were being presented on the screen of pure consciousness.

As he focused more intently, however, his confusion vanished and he realized that he was in samadhi. His consciousness had transcended the realm of time and space and he was being blessed with the intuitive experience of his sanchita karmas. All of his previous lives were before him and there was no distinction between them and his present life. It was as if the past had slipped into the present and the present had walked into the past.

Allowing his consciousness to expand further, he traveled deeper into the backyard of time. The more he searched, the more he discovered about himself. This experience was shocking. He was overwhelmed by the numberless life-forms he had assumed in the past. He had been a king, a beggar, an insect, an elephant, a demon, a celestial being, and everything in between. He had hurt others, and others had hurt him. He saw millions of individual souls—some he had hated, and they had hated him; some he had loved, and they had loved him. Everything that had ever happened to him had created an impression, and all of these impressions had been stored intact. Although there were occasional intervals of pleasure, a stream of vivid pain flowed continuously throughout all these experiences. Before entering this state he had not been aware of those deposited impressions, nor had he been affected by them. But now he saw quite clearly that they would eventually manifest. This realization forced him to ponder issues he had never thought he would entertain.

"How and why did I involve myself in this apparently unending chain of karmas?" he wondered. "How vast our unconscious mind is to be able to accommodate all these karmic seeds! What force preserves these seeds and allows them to sprout and grow at specific times, causing them to manifest as destiny? Not all these dormant karmas are awakened at once. Who decides which particular group is to be activated?" Overwhelmed by the sheer number of his dormant karmas, Jaigishavya grew discouraged. He realized that at some point they would gather momentum and become active, pushing him to migrate from one form of life to another.

"I am able to see the history of millions of lifetimes of my transmigration," he thought, "but I still can't see the beginning of my soul's outward journey. This means there are still dormant karmas lying beyond my present intuitive capacity. I can do nothing about the dormant karmas that are outside my awareness—but do I have the freedom to erase, rewrite, throw away, or recycle the dormant karmas I have identified? If so, how can it be done?"

While Jaigishavya was tangled in the maze of his own self-discovery, one of the immortal guides, the sage Avatya, sensed that someone was in need of his help. This sage, working on behalf of the primordial master, Bhagavan Narayana, aids advanced seekers who have become stuck at such a high level that neither the scriptures nor teachers in human form can help them. Even though they are always connected with the cosmic mind (hiranyagarbha), the sages on this level are also connected with the mind of each individual.

Intent on cutting asunder the yogi's final knot of ignorance, sage Avatya emerged from the universal pool of consciousness and descended into Jaigishavya's consciousness. Jaigishavya prostrated before him, and sage Avatya lifted him lovingly and spoke: "You have been overwhelmed by discovering the vastnesss of your karmic field. Tell me, how can I help you?"

Jaigishavya replied, "It is disheartening that after my long dedication to intense yogic practices I still have so many karmas stored in my mind. And even after knowing they are there, I do not know how to get rid of them."

Sage Avatya replied, "Because of your austerities and your practice of meditation, you were able to penetrate your own *chitta,* the vast unconscious mind where the subtle impressions of all your past deeds are stored. You are consciously experiencing your unconscious. You think you are witnessing the contents of your mind while remaining above it, but you are not; you are actively involved. That is maya. Rise above maya and you will see what or who lies beyond."

"O Ocean of Compassion, how can I rise above maya?"

"The first step in tearing the veil of maya," Avatya explained, "is to sharpen your intellect so that you can clearly understand why you are attracted to knowing your past. Your interest in your past is an indication of your desire to reclaim it. And this desire to reclaim the past is due to your attachment. You are aware that most of your past is painful. Logically, you should have no desire to reassociate yourself with painful events, yet you are drawn to them. Why? Because you are attached to your actions, the fruits of your actions, and their subtle impressions. You treasure them in your mindfield, although you know how useless, ugly, and painful they are. That is how sanchita karmas gather their momentum and come into manifestation.

"People are drawn to painful, disgusting, and violent stories because such stories help them reassociate with their past thoughts, memories, and ideas. This reassociation engenders a sense of pleasure. Just as worldly people listen to such stories for pleasure, spiritual people find pleasure in experiencing them in samadhi. They call it 'storytelling,' you call it a 'spiritual experience,' but it is essentially the same process. By listening to these tales, worldly people awaken and act out their subtle impressions. If the impressions are strong, they are deeply affected. As a result they may commit themselves to take a related action, thus creating more karmas. That is how their dormant sanchita karmas turn into prarabdha karmas, which are the fabric of destiny.

"If you are negligent, this conscious experience of your unconscious can trick you. In fact, it has already tricked you. You are reassociating yourself with your dormant karmas by brooding on them and by figuring out when, how, and why you created them in the first place."

Avatya saw that Jaigishavya was growing more troubled. "Let me help you," the sage said gently. "I will properly formulate the questions which are already in your mind in a hodgepodge state. This will help you contemplate on them and find the answers.

"Tell me, how many karmas do you have? Do you remember when you performed your first action, reaped its fruit, and stored the impression in your mind? When did it become active and motivate you to perform the next set of actions? When did you become aware of the cycle of karmic action— from active karma, to potential, to dormant, and back to active again?"

Jaigishavya replied, "Sir, I do not know how many karmas I have stored in dormant form nor when I performed my first action. Nor do I know how or when I created these impressions. And I have even less of an idea how the wheel of karma was set in motion."

"Then tell me," sage Avatya asked, "can you categorize your dormant karmas?"

"Yes. Dormant karmas are either painful or pleasant, undesirable or desirable, hard to deal with or easy to deal with."

"Now tell me, which category of dormant karmas is larger: the painful, or the pleasant?"

"The painful," replied Jaigishavya. "Even the pleasant ones are contaminated by pain. Even a pleasant memory makes me emotional, because there is a desire to recapture the pleasant moments—but the past is past, and that is painful."

Sage Avatya smiled and said, "This answer is the result of your deep analysis and introspection. When I arrived you were simply recounting your sanchita karmas. Now you have gained some perspective. Reinforce it by contemplating on this truth: all samskaras are painful. All beings caught in the karmic whirlpool are bound to experience pain. Disidentify from your karmas.

"You had been reinforcing the idea that you were a doer of actions. Your anxiety about the fruits of action made you miserable while you performed actions. In the event that you did not achieve the desired results, your disappointment made you miserable; your worry about retaining the fruits of your actions also made you miserable. In this way every action you have ever taken was smeared with the impressions of misery. You must understand that every karma, to some degree, contains inherent misery. True knowledge lies not in knowing your karmas but rather in knowing their inherent nature. This type of knowledge will give you freedom from the effects of your dormant karmas."

For some time, Avatya continued his instruction. "Whenever a memory either grieves or thrills you," the sage warned, "it is your attachment giving energy to that related dormant karma. Instantly neutralize that karma with the power of nonattachment.

"Attachment," he explained, "is like the nutrients a seed needs in order to sprout. Once you no longer provide these nutrients, the seed of dormant karma will lose its capacity to grow into destiny. But some of the dormant karmas are so strong that even if you do not have any attachment to them at a conscious level, they still find a way to manifest as destiny. In relation to such powerful karmas it is not enough to simply remain unattached to them. The practice of nonattachment is a passive preventive measure. It works only in relation to weak karmas.

"To neutralize the effect of powerful dormant karmas," the sage continued, "you must commit yourself to a methodical practice, and that practice has to be intense. During such a practice you have to summon your entire *sankalpa shakti,* the power of will and determination, to complete it regardless of how many obstacles you may face. Thus *vairagya* [nonattachment] and *abhyasa* [practice] are the ways to attain freedom from your dormant karmas."

After imparting this knowledge, Avatya disappeared. Jaigishavya's confusion and discouragement had been dispelled, and he redoubled his commitment to spiritual disciplines. He persevered until one day he became *yogishvara,* lord of the yogis—completely free from all karmas and their fruits.

———

In light of this story, let's revisit the stories in chapter one. Masters like Sri Swami Sadanand and Swamiji (Sri Swami Rama) have the ability to penetrate subtle realms of our being, where both dormant and active karmas reside. If we have the good karma to be in their company and catch their attention, these masters show us how to neutralize undesirable sanchita karmas before they gather their momentum and manifest in the form of prarabdha, or destiny.

In the case of my mother's loss of vision, her dormant karmas were awakened and manifested as destiny. It was too late for medicines. She needed help from an extraordinary source—the sun, which is the eye of the universe. My mother did not know the *aditya hridayam* mantra nor did she have the ability to undertake the practice of it. Although I had both, I was young and immature, and my simple recitation of it could not have been the cause underlying the restoration of her eyesight. Rather, just as a teacher transmits the power of mantra by blessing the student during mantra initiation, the invisible force of Sri Sadanandji's blessings served as a medium between my mother and the healing power of the aditya hridayam mantra, in which this gentle saint was proficient. (*Aditya hridayam* means "the heart of the sun.") A new karmic force created by the mantra blocked the flow of prarabdha karmas and neutralized the remaining karmas, which were still in their sanchita form. In this way, my mother was healed in three days.

In the case of the man with epilepsy, Swami Sadanandji guided him to stop the further spread of the karmas manifesting as his destiny by practicing selfless service. Through this he created a set of new karmas as an antidote to the pain of epilepsy. The same was true when the saint caused the young man to miss his train. By serving someone who was always in the service of God, the young man neutralized his dormant karmas that would have manifested as destiny the next day if the saint had not taken him under his wing (although we do not know whether this karma was destroyed forever or simply postponed).

The incident involving Laura is more complicated. I had no clue that I would be in an accident on that particular day. How much Swamiji knew about it, he alone knows. But the experience allows me to say with certainty that I was quite close to death or terrible injury. The practice that Swamiji gave me to do in Rishikesh aims to induce victory over death and disease. The protective force I saw in a reverie-like state both during the practice and during the actual event was intangible but visible. We could come up with several interpretations of this experience and its relationship with karma, but all of them would simply give rise to further questions, and in any case the riddle of Laura's change in behavior remains unsolved. However, we can surmise that through mantra practice, prayer, and the blessings of the blessed ones, dormant karmas can be altered or neutralized.

Active Karma (Prarabdha)

The karmas of destiny, active karmas, are hard to change. They are like arrows already in flight, and because they run at the speed of time, it is almost impossible to change their direction. The laws governing prarabdha karma are similar to Newton's first and second laws of motion. Newton's first law states that an object moving in a straight line will continue in a straight line unless acted upon by an outside force. An object in motion will stay in motion, and an object at rest will stay at rest, unless an outside force acts on it. This is known as the principle of inertia—for a force to change an object's motion, it must first overcome the inertia of the object. The same is true of the karmas that constitute our destiny. They will continue to move in a particular direction at a set rate of speed unless acted upon by an outside force.

According to Newton's second law, an object changes its motion when a force is applied to it; the change of motion depends on the magnitude of the force and the mass of the object. The greater an object's mass, the harder it is to put the object into motion or change its velocity; thus the change in motion of a heavy object will be less under a given applied force than the change in motion of a lighter object.

In yogic literature we find tales and parables about karmic predicaments. In some, great masters and even divine incarnations could not overcome the inertia of active karmas: in spite of knowing the details of someone's destiny, they could not influence either its direction or its speed. In other cases, they changed the direction, slowed it down, or stopped it entirely, thus helping someone to escape before destiny could strike. The following stories will illustrate the dynamics of prarabdha karma.

About four hundred years ago a man named Maluk Das lived on the plains of northern India. He was fully absorbed in farming and raising cattle and had no time to participate in religious activities. His simple life occupied him completely, and he never thought about larger issues. He did not even know if he believed in God, destiny, or rebirth.

One hot, humid morning he decided to rest for a while. It was *adhik mas,* a month that devout Hindus dedicate to reading scriptures, chanting, and meditating. A local pandit was reciting scriptures under a tree, drawing a small crowd of villagers, and Maluk Das joined them.

In the course of the recitation the pandit said, "Destiny is inevitable. We must experience the pleasure or pain brought about by destiny; there is no other way. If, due to our karma, we are supposed to be happy, we will be happy. If we are supposed to be miserable, we will be miserable. We cannot go hungry if we are supposed to have food. A human being has no freedom of choice, but must undergo whatever destiny has in store."

Maluk Das was intrigued, so he challenged the pandit: "Are you saying this just because it is written in that book, or do you have proof?"

Evidently the pandit had some intuitive knowledge, for he replied, "The proof is this: today you are not supposed to be hungry. No matter what you do, you will be fed."

Maluk Das took this as a challenge. "I am not going to eat, no matter what comes," he said. "An action cannot be performed unless someone performs it. And the performer of an action has freedom of choice. Today I will prove it to you."

Proud of his decision, Maluk Das left the gathering. It was almost time for his lunch. He was determined not to eat, so he avoided the village and made his way to the dense forest nearby, where he hid in the branches of a tall tree and settled down to wait for evening. Soon he heard voices. They grew progressively louder, until they were right under his tree. Peering through the branches, Maluk Das saw three men making plates from the leaves of the tree he was hiding in. They washed their hands in the nearby stream, put food on the plates, and were about to begin their meal when a tiger suddenly roared nearby. In a panic, the travelers jumped over the stream and vanished into the forest beyond, leaving their meal behind.

Maluk Das suspected that the pandit had arranged this scene to entice him into eating, but this only steeled his determination not to be tricked. He settled himself more firmly amid the branches and continued to wait. In a little while, three more men stopped under his tree. From their looks and their talk, he concluded that they were robbers. "How gracious is God," said one. "Even in such a deep forest, he takes care of us. No one other than God would serve meals to the likes of us."

"Don't be foolish," another one said. "Someone might be chasing us and trying to kill us. I'm sure this food has been poisoned." The third one said, "I think you're right. And my guess is that the person is somewhere nearby. Let's find him and feed this food to him—that'll teach him a lesson."

So the three robbers set out to find the person who had left the food. Soon one of them noticed Maluk Das hiding in the branches. He called his confederates and together they forced Maluk Das from the tree. The farmer tried to explain why he was there, but naturally the robbers didn't believe him. They gave him a couple of slaps and then two of them pushed him down and opened his jaws, while the third pushed food into his mouth, making sure that he ate from each of the plates. Then they kept him captive for a while to see whether or not he showed signs of being poisoned. Once they were sure the food was pure, they ate the rest and let him go.

By the time Maluk Das returned to the village, it was almost dark. The next day he found the pandit, gained further knowledge, and committed himself to spiritual practice. Eventually he became one of the greatest saints in north India. Kade Ki Mai, a famous temple of the Divine Mother associated with saint Maluk Das, still stands today near the city of Allahabad.

———

This story shows the relentless power of destiny. Maluk Das' prarabdha karma was so strong that he could not change it, in spite of his best efforts. His main karma was that he must eat, and his secondary karmas led to the events that resulted in his taking a meal. From his standpoint both the travelers and the robbers were instruments in the hands of his destiny. Maluk Das could not apply a force strong enough to overcome the inertia of his destiny, and it continued on in the direction it was going. The next story, which appears in the Puranas, gives us another glimpse of destiny's power.

———

Once there was a beggar who wasn't very successful at his occupation. Even after begging all day long, he hardly ever got enough to eat, so he was always half starved. One day Parvati, the wife of Lord Shiva, noticed the beggar's misery, and, deeply moved, she asked Shiva to help him.

"O Parvati," Shiva replied, "poverty and prosperity, misery and joy, and other undesirable and desirable conditions in life are the result of one's destiny. It cannot be changed. No matter what you do, this poor fellow cannot be helped."

But Parvati argued, "O Lord, you are omniscient and capable of doing anything you wish. Besides, the law of love and compassion is stronger than the law of karma. Why should a divine being like you ignore this man just because he does not have good prarabdha karma? If a person is not in the position to help himself, that is all the more reason for others to help. Please help him."

The warmth of his beloved wife's entreaty made Shiva relent. "Tell me, in what manner do you want me to help him?"

"Lord, make him rich," she implored. "Put a big heap of gold coins on the road that he walks every day."

"So be it," said Shiva.

Immediately a heap of gold appeared on the road just ahead of the beggar.

At the same moment, the beggar thought, "I wonder how blind people walk? How do they manage? Let me try it and find out." So the beggar closed his eyes and passed by the gold without seeing it.

Parvati turned to Shiva. "Lord, give him one more chance. It was an accident that he started thinking that way. Please, use your intuitive power to place the coins precisely at the spot where he is supposed to step, even if his eyes are closed."

"As you wish, Parvati," Shiva replied, and with precise calculation he placed the heap of gold right in the beggar's path. At that very moment the beggar was struck by another whim. "I have seen some blind people walking without a stick," he mused. "Sometimes they even take big leaps. I wonder how they do that?" With that thought, he threw his walking stick aside and started taking large jumps forward. So it was that he jumped over the gold and was very happy with his accomplishment.

"See, Parvati," said Shiva. "His destiny is so heavy and is moving with such speed that neither you nor I can stop it. Don't you remember that when King Nala was suffering from poverty, even the roasted fish he was about to consume ended up back in the river? Let us go and help where our efforts can bear fruit."

So Shiva and Parvati departed.

By its very nature destiny is entrenched and almost insur-
mountable. Yet in some cases it can be altered if enough force
is applied—and in a skillful enough manner—as the next tale
illustrates.

———

There once was a brahmin couple. They were learned but
quite poor—their only property was a horse. They did not
own any land, so the only way they could feed the horse was to
cut grass with the permission of the landowner or try to get
some from the overgrazed public lands.

Every day the wife searched for grass for the horse while the
husband went from door to door looking for a tutoring job—
usually to no avail. Poverty and hunger aged the couple
rapidly, although the horse was healthy and strong, due
to their kindness and care.

One hot summer day the great sage Narada visited the village and stopped at the couple's door for alms. Even though
they were embarrassed at not being able to provide a meal,
they greeted him warmly, offering him salt and water, which
was all they had. When the couple explained their situation,
Narada looked into their prarabdha karmas and found that
the only property their destiny held for them was this one
horse. He also checked their dormant karmas and saw there
were hundreds of horses lined up, although none would manifest until the current horse was gone.

So Narada told them to sell the horse. They were reluctant,
but they knew Narada wouldn't advise them to do anything
not in their best interest. The sage also told them that since the
husband was a learned brahmin, his first duty was to dissemi-
nate knowledge. He should start a school so that he could
house and teach students right in his own home. In this way

the couple would free themselves from the burden of caring for a horse and knocking on doors looking for students to tutor.

With Narada's help the horse was sold by the end of the day. The couple bought food and announced that the brahmin would take in students. People were amazed, for they knew how much the couple loved their horse. The sale was interpreted in all kinds of ways, but most people concluded that all these years they had failed to recognize the couple's greatness and generosity. The villagers believed that the couple had sold their prized possession for the sake of providing education to others. People began whispering among themselves, saying, "Shame on us for not respecting their selfless love. We thought they were a burden. We should honor them."

Taking this to heart, someone soon donated a horse to the brahmin. Following Narada's instructions, he promptly sold it and used the proceeds to expand the school. Almost immediately someone else donated another horse, which the brahmin also sold. Convinced of the brahmin's greatness and selflessness, the villagers wanted to make sure that he always had a horse, so each time he sold one, another was donated. The school continued to expand; although the couple's property was still limited to one horse, their poverty vanished, never to return, and they lived a graceful, happy life.

———

Here destiny was not averted, but skillfully altered. Narada's guidance and the couple's faith in the sage enabled them to act on his instructions and engendered a force greater than the force of destiny—which in this case had induced poverty. Moreover, the same force helped overcome the inertia that kept their dormant karmas at rest, and these karmas began turning into destiny faster than they would have if that force had not been applied.

Potential Karma (Kriyamana)

Potential karmas are like arrows that have not yet been made, although the factory, the skilled arrow maker, the raw materials, and the customer are all present. The ego is the factory, the senses are the arrow makers, anxiety is the raw material, and the desire-ridden mind is the consumer. It is up to our faculty of discrimination to make the final decision as to whether or not these arrows will be made. If they are, they will be stored as dormant (sanchita) karmas, and sooner or later they are bound to be shot, resulting in destiny—prarabdha karma.

Kriyamana (potential) karmas are in our hands, provided we have the knowledge and ability to exercise our faculty of discrimination properly. Although our present level of knowledge and ability are greatly influenced by our active karmas, as human beings we have a high degree of free will and the power of choice. We are blessed with the ability to think linearly, as well as with the power of discrimination. By using these gifts we can avoid creating undesirable potential karmas, and we can create potential karmas which can soon neutralize the impact of our negative dormant karmas and even of our destiny. The *Srimad Bhagavatam* provides a story that clarifies this process.

————

Angira and Narada are two of the most mysterious sages in the Vedic tradition, and both are famous for guiding students at levels incomprehensible to ordinary minds.

One day these two sages visited the palace of King Chitra Ketu, and were greeted by the learned king and his many queens. The sages inquired into the health and happiness of the royal family and the welfare of the kingdom. The king replied, "There is peace, prosperity, and contentment throughout the kingdom. The clouds bring rain on time and our crops grow in abundance. There is such great moral strength and inner contentment among the citizens that there is little need for authorities to maintain order. But in spite of this, merciful sages, my heart is empty. I am growing old and I am without a child. The thought of dying without leaving my kingdom in the hands of a worthy successor makes me miserable."

"Life is a mystery," Angira replied. "It is a mingled stream of joy and sorrow. But deep within lies a real and everlasting joy. A human being is born to dive deep into the stream of life, find the hidden treasure, and attain eternal fulfillment."

"O compassionate Angira, I understand what you are saying," the king answered. "But still this desire lingers in my mind day and night. Once it is fulfilled, I will pursue the path of eternal peace with a composed and tranquil mind. O sages, I beg you for a son."

But Angira countered: "It does not befit a learned person like you to work against destiny, especially if it is already working in your favor. It is easy to serve others selflessly when you do not have self-interest. It is very hard to overcome desire and attachment to one's own children. When you achieve something in the normal course of your destiny, you may not develop a strong attachment toward that object. But when you gain it after a struggle, you value it too highly; if it should be destroyed, your emotions are deeply stirred. My advice is that you surrender to your destiny. Drop your desire for a child and pursue the highest goal of life."

But the king could not be persuaded. "I am already so miserable that I can hardly think of anything else," he said. "How can I pursue a spiritual path in this state of mind? Once this desire has been fulfilled and the kingdom has been entrusted to my rightful heir, I will gladly follow the path of renunciation."

Finally, out of compassion Angira relented, saying, "May you be blessed with a son."

Then, with foresight, Narada added: "This child will be the cause of both joy and misery."

A few months later the king was delighted to find that one of his queens had conceived, and when the baby was born there was rejoicing throughout the kingdom. But as the proud father began to spend more and more time with the infant and his mother, the other queens grew jealous. And as the king's involvement with his son and his mother continued to deepen, it fueled the jealousy of the childless queens until they were so enraged that they poisoned the young prince.

The terrible news struck the king to the heart, and his grief overpowered him. Well-wishers and wise men offered condolences, but to no avail. Days passed, and the king remained distraught. His counselors made him feel worse—their condolences were like salt in a grievous wound. Each expression of sympathy awakened his memories anew.

After some time, Angira and Narada appeared again, but the king was so disoriented by his intense sorrow that he failed to recognize them. Still, their mere presence healed his tormented heart. He felt as though they had brought a cooling breeze that gently swept away his grief, so he sensed that there was something remarkable about them.

"Who are you?" he asked. "Your presence has healed my wounds. Please make yourselves known so I may honor you."

"I am Angira," the sage replied, "and this is Narada. We came some time ago to give you the highest gift of knowledge, but you were not ready for it. Your desire to have a son was so strong that we could not help you. You were convinced that you could set foot on the path of the highest good only after your desires were fulfilled."

At these words, the king fell at their feet and asked humbly, "What does it all mean? Why is there pain in life and in all the relationships that are a part of this life? Where does real peace lie—inside or outside of this world? Why is everything so disappointing? Help me, please. I am at your feet."

Angira answered, "I told you before that life is a mystery. Experiences, both pleasant or painful, manifesting in the present, are the result of our destiny. Active karmas determine when, where, and how we will be born; how long we live in that body; and what major events we will face in that lifetime. In regard to this group of karmas, we cannot do very much.

"But stocked in the deepest recesses of our unconscious mind is another set of karmas, the dormant ones. They are numberless. In the journey of many lifetimes we have performed so many actions and have reaped so many fruits that we have stored the impressions of all kinds of karmas. It is possible to awaken any of them and allow them to manifest in the present in the form of active karma, provided we have a strong desire to awaken them.

"That is what happened to you. Destiny had not planned a son for you in this lifetime. By being content without a son, you could have played out your destiny and attained freedom from the bondage of karma. But your strong desire forced you to search for a son in the storehouse of dormant karmas, and this storehouse abides in a deeper realm than the prarabdha karmas which constitute your destiny. In that storehouse the only dormant karmas which could give you a son were contaminated with pain and misery."

Bewildered, the king asked, "If you knew this, why did you give me your blessing to have a child?"

"We were your guests," Angira explained. "You served us lovingly and respectfully. You had been our student for a long time, and due to your service we were bound to give you something. We offered you the knowledge of nonattachment, but you preferred a son. As your teacher, Narada warned you that your son would be the cause of both joy and misery, but your strong desire did not allow you to heed his voice.

"It was our duty to guide you in the right direction, but in spite of our advice you insisted on a son. So after a strong warning, we gave you the kind of blessing you asked for. This was the result of your potential karma. You created it and you alone are responsible for it."

The king understood. "I surrender myself to you," he said. "Please guide me. What should I do to stop being miserable?"

"*Vairagya* [dispassion] is the only way," Angira replied. "With the help of *vairagya* you can shun the aftereffect of your loss. Lack of dispassion forces you to cling to the object of your desire, and this clinging becomes the cause of anger, hatred, confusion, loss of memory, and ultimately the loss of your power of discrimination. In such a mental state you will not be able to stop from creating another long chain of potential karma, thus adding momentum to the cycle of karma in which you are already caught.

"But once you are established in *vairagya* your mind will become peaceful and your senses will be under control. Your awareness will turn inward. Your mind will accompany you all the time, like a benevolent friend. You may then continue to perform your actions, but you will also have time to pursue your higher goals."

Narada then described how the force of providence guides those who are karmically connected, pulling them into situations that automatically create a worldly bond that is either pleasant or unpleasant. "Such bonds exist for a while and then vanish," Narada added. "A person with true wisdom remains steadfast throughout all the phases of relationships: when the bonds are first forged; when the resulting karma blossoms and disperses the aroma of either pleasure or pain; and when those bonds are shattered. Throughout these cycles, the one who has true wisdom does not spend his time and energy wallowing in emotional turmoil. Thus he is free from loss and gain."

The king then asked, "How can I avoid making such mistakes in the future? How can I avoid trapping myself in potential karmas, especially those which invite a long chain of misery?"

"The mind is powerful and volatile, easily led by desires or worries," the sage replied. "At the unconscious level, it knows what kind of karmas and subtle impressions are stored inside, but out of curiosity, anxiety, and attachment it is drawn to the hidden impressions from the past. Because many of our desires are linked to our past karmas, attachment to these past karmas is ever present. Therefore, although we may not be aware of it at the conscious level, these impressions trigger our thought processes, and when they do, at a subtle level we begin to think about the objects associated with our past karmas. This awakens our attachment to those objects. Once awakened, the desire for these objects grows. In response to those desires, we perform actions and end up with kriyamana karmas."

"But how can we prevent these potential karmas from being created in the first place?" asked the king.

"There is much you can do to prevent yourself from creating potential karmas that are not conducive to your spiritual growth," Narada answered. Then he gave the king the following guidelines:

Renounce desire and attachment, as well as the company of those who are filled with desire and attachment.

Seek the company of wise people and embrace their teachings in your thought, speech, and action.

Remember that nothing in this world belongs to you. You can use the objects of the world presented by your destiny, but at some point you must leave them behind in order to walk forward.

Form the habit of living in solitude, for only there can you contemplate on the higher reality without distraction.

Cut asunder your worldly relationships once you have fulfilled your duties and obligations.

Do not identify yourself as the doer of actions that your personality traits drive you to perform.

Renounce the fruits of your actions and rise above the dance of duality: success and failure, loss and gain, honor and insult, reward and punishment, and so on.

"By embracing these instructions," Narada told the king, "you will perform your actions without being motivated by desire and attachment. Such karmas become impotent—they have no power to sprout."

Under the guidance of Angira and Narada, King Chitra Ketu made a firm decision to follow the path of light. Through intense sadhana and by practicing dispassion *(vairagya)* his worldview was transformed, and ultimately he attained complete freedom from his karmic deeds.

As this story indicates, in certain areas of life we have little or no freedom of choice—some events are totally in the hands of destiny. King Chitra Ketu would not have been able to beget a son through his self-effort alone. He got a son only through the intervention of the sages Angira and Narada, yet even the blessings of these great sages could not entirely alter the course of his destiny. For a short period the king was graced with a child, but soon he fell into the stream of his central prarabdha karma, which destined him to remain childless. His desire, which was the potential karma that enabled him to awaken his dormant karmas for having a son, brought grief along with it.

King Chitra Ketu's plight also shows us that the main strand of destiny is usually surrounded and supported by numberless secondary karmas. The main prarabdha karma acts like a magnet; the secondary karmas are pulled toward it like iron filings. Because it is difficult to separate the secondary karmas from the main prarabdha karmas, they usually work in perfect coordination, mutually supporting one another.

The same is true of dormant karmas. A powerful dormant karma is usually surrounded by many secondary dormant karmas. When the main one is awakened and becomes destiny, the secondary ones are automatically awakened. That is why learned masters tell us that unless we know the complete mystery and dynamics of karma, it is better not to try to alter it. Divine grace flows along with the current of destiny, and it is this grace that gives us the strength to withstand the storms stirred up by our karmas.

Situations and circumstances which we cannot change are part of our destiny. It is best to honor such circumstances and accept them as they are. If you have the wisdom and ability to transform them for the better, go ahead—but make sure you do it without violating the laws of nature. Nature is the highest repository of each individual's destiny, and it gives you only what you need. If you attempt to neutralize or modify your destiny, you must take care not to mistake your desires for your needs. Even if you come in touch with the divine providence that operates beyond the law of destiny, do not ask for more than you can sustain.

Even wise people obey the law of destiny. When absolutely necessary they may modify it slightly, although they are careful not to dishonor it when they do so. Lord Krishna demonstrated this beautifully when he was serving as Arjuna's chariot driver in the *Mahabharata* war.

———

Several years earlier, Arjuna had burned a great forest to propitiate the god of fire. A very special family of snakes had been living in that forest for thousands of years, and the fire killed all except one. This lone survivor dedicated his life to avenging the death of his family by striking at Arjuna. He knew that he could not take his revenge in face-to-face combat. He also knew that there was only one warrior in the entire land equal to Arjuna: Karna, who was also Arjuna's staunch enemy. And he knew he could never kill Arjuna without Karna's help. So the snake approached the warrior and offered his assistance, but Karna refused it. He wanted to defeat Arjuna without anyone's help.

Several years later the snake died, but not his desire for revenge. This was so strong that even after his death his consciousness continued to search for a means of vengeance. And this desire, together with the snake's firm belief in Karna's ability to kill Arjuna in combat, brought his soul to dwell in one of Karna's arrows.

When Karna and Arjuna found themselves face to face on the battlefield, Karna shot this special arrow. Because it was imbued with the force of the snake's vengeance, it was certain to hit the target. Karna had aimed precisely at Arjuna's forehead. Lord Krishna, who was Arjuna's chariot driver as well as his protector and guide, was aware that it was Arjuna's destiny to be struck by the snake. The arrow was already in flight. In a flash, Krishna made the horses kneel, causing the chariot bed to dip a few inches. At that instant the arrow turned into the snake and struck, hitting Arjuna's gold crown instead of his forehead.

Krishna had the capacity to alter the destiny of everyone concerned. He could have changed the mind of the snake; he could have destroyed the arrow imbued with the snake's consciousness; he could have spoiled Karna's aim; he could even have made Arjuna's body arrow-proof. But he did not. He honored destiny by allowing it to manifest completely. At the last moment, he employed his skill with horses to save Arjuna. This was his duty as a chariot driver.

———

Stories such as the ones in this chapter lead us to understand that the law of karma has been set by nature with divine guidance. Under normal circumstances this law cannot be violated—I have never found a single example of a great master who tried to change his or her own destiny. Masters always work with their dormant and potential karma and honor destiny in its current form. When moved by their inherent compassion and kindness, enlightened masters consider changing another person's sanchita or prarabdha karmas only after they have taken the will of the Divine into account.

It is important for us to have at least a rudimentary understanding of the threefold karmas and their interrelationship, but this is not enough to enable us to develop a plan for attaining mastery over them. To do that, we need to understand the force that causes karmas to be formed, to be stored intact, and finally to manifest in the realm of time and space. This leads us to study the mind, for according to the yogis, that is where this karmic drama is created, enacted, and experienced.

CHAPTER THREE

HOW THE MIND CREATES KARMAS

ACCORDING TO YOGA SCIENCE, everything in the universe, including the mind, has evolved from *prakriti* (primordial nature). Prakriti is eternal and all-pervading. It is the cause of our manifest world. Itself unborn, it is the mother of the entire universe and all that exists in it. It is the highest form of energy. The energy of prakriti, for example, is more refined than electricity, magnetism, and gravity. (According to yoga, these forces belong to the manifest world and are not energy at all, but subtle forms of matter.) Prakriti has three intrinsic forces: *sattva, rajas,* and *tamas.* While prakriti is in its unmanifest form, these intrinsic forces remain in perfect balance. When this balance is disturbed, prakriti becomes manifest.

Everything in the manifest world consists of sattva, rajas, and tamas in varying degrees. Sattva is the force characterized by light, illumination, upward movement, clarity, purity, warmth, and inspiration. Rajas is the force of activity, movement, instability, agitation, and pulsation. Tamas is the force of darkness, heaviness, inertia, downward movement, confusion, sloth, dullness, and lack of enthusiasm. Sattva and tamas appear to be opposites, while rajas is the force of activity or animation. Due to rajas, vibration is an intrinsic characteristic of prakriti.

Unlike the vibrations evident in the material world, the vibration in prakriti has neither a cause nor a medium through which to vibrate. As long as sattva, rajas, and tamas are in equilibrium, this basic principle of vibration remains still. But once this equilibrium is disturbed, there ensues a primordial explosion of all the pairs of opposites, causing the objective world to emerge in all its diversity.

The mind—both the cosmic mind and the individual mind—is the first to emerge from the stillness of prakriti; the material world then evolves from the mind. According to the yogic doctrine of evolution, an effect must contain all the qualities and characteristics of its cause, and it cannot have qualities and characteristics which do not exist in its cause. Because prakriti is the mother of the mind, the mind consists of the three forces intrinsic to prakriti. If these forces reach a perfect state of equilibrium, the mind will no longer exist as such but will be merged in prakriti.

By the same token, as long as the mind exists, these forces cannot be in perfect equilibrium. It is the nature of the mind to be dominated by either sattva or rajas or tamas, while the other two forces are subordinate. The interplay of these three forces causes the mind to continually shift from one state to another, which is why it never functions in a perfectly balanced manner. By turns and in varying degrees it is distracted, stupefied, disturbed, one-pointed, or well controlled.

A well-controlled mind emerges when sattva is the dominant force, and both rajas and tamas are minimal. When rajas
and tamas increase proportionately and the dominance
of sattva declines slightly, the mind slips from a perfectly
controlled state into relative one-pointedness. When rajas
and tamas have increased to the point at which sattva is only
slightly stronger than they are, the mind becomes disturbed.
When tamas is the dominant force and rajas and sattva are
subservient, the mind becomes stupefied. When rajas dominates, the mind falls into a distracted state. The mind usually
remains in one or more of the first three states—distracted,
stupefied, or disturbed—only occasionally becoming one-
pointed, and rarely, if ever, well controlled.

Because our thoughts, speech, and actions are either confused, organized, or peaceful, depending on our mental state,
these mental states play a significant role in the formation of
our karmas. In a distracted, stupefied, or disturbed state of
mind, for example, our actions as well as their fruits are confused. Actions performed under the influence of a confused
mind will be accompanied by samskaras (subtle impressions)
of confusion, and their results will be confused as well. Even if
these actions and their impressions are positive, they will still
be contaminated with confusion. A confused mind causes us to
create a multitude of weak karmas, which in turn are stored in
the unconscious mind in a disorganized way.

Creating Samskaras

To get a clearer understanding of this, let us look at how
two people—one whose mind is disturbed and one whose
mind is one-pointed—might handle the same situation. Both

are professionals and both like chocolate. They each face a decision about which chocolate bar to buy—an innocuous decision, but one which clearly demonstrates the workings and interplay of the various kinds of karma.

In our first example, a freelance computer consultant— we'll call him Fred—is working at home. His wife has gone to her office, dropping the children at school on the way. Early in the afternoon Fred gets a call from a customer who is furious because a defect in Fred's work is causing problems with his software. The customer insists that the problem be fixed immediately, and Fred agrees to come right over. But the moment he hangs up, the phone rings again. The school is calling to say a blizzard is expected and he should pick up his children. Intent on keeping the appointment with his customer, Fred calls his wife to ask her to pick up the children, but to his dismay she tells him she is having a problem with her car and needs a ride home herself.

Because he cannot refuse any of these requests, he becomes agitated as he tries to figure out how to get his family home safely and still get to his customer's office. So he first picks up the children. They are cranky and demand some computer games to entertain them during the blizzard. The game store is next to the supermarket and both are on the way to his wife's office. He decides to stop and let the kids get their games while he picks up milk and other items the family will need to ride out the storm.

On his way to the dairy case, Fred passes through the candy aisle. Chocolate is his favorite food, so he stops without thinking. There are twenty different kinds of chocolate bars on display. He had no intention of buying chocolate when he came into the store, but his mind is so scattered and the chocolate bars so captivating that he starts looking at them. He can see all twenty different varieties of chocolate clearly; eighteen grab his attention because he is familiar with them. Should he buy them or not? He doesn't want to buy all of them, so which ones should he pass over? His favorite, imported from Belgium, is on sale, but he already has a good supply of them at home. After looking again and again at the different packages, he eliminates two more but still finds himself attracted to fifteen. That is still too many. He looks again and finally grabs four at random and drops them into his cart. He looks around. He is so harried and confused that he has no idea where to go next. He can't even remember why he is in the store. With an effort he reorients himself, collects the groceries he planned to buy, and goes next door to get the children.

Now let us analyze the chocolate karmas Fred created in that confused state of mind, what kind they were, and how those karmas were stored in his memory-field and became samskaras. At the sensory level, he noticed the existence of twenty different kinds of chocolate. At this first level, none of these chocolates were good or bad, expensive or inexpensive, more or less desirable. The subtle impressions of chocolates at this stage were vague and accompanied by uncertainty and aimlessness. Let's call this first level "chocolate samskara 1." Then Fred focused his attention, distinguished one chocolate from another, and recognized their characteristics—superior, inferior, expensive, cheap, unknown, and so on. This is Fred's "chocolate samskara 2." He then began to analyze the chocolates further. He identified eighteen of them. Based on his previous experiences, a sense of liking and disliking arose from this identification. The memories associated with those eighteen varieties of chocolate rushed forward, forcing him to buy chocolate. But still there were too many different kinds. With this feeling, which is accompanied with identification and judgment, he stored these eighteen varieties in his memory-field as "chocolate samskara 3."

Next Fred transferred the chocolate file to the decisive faculty of his mind (known as *buddhi*) to make a final decision about which to buy. But the buddhi was confused too. The best variety according to the decisive faculty was the one imported from Belgium. But another thought flashed: "There is a lot of it in our refrigerator; I probably shouldn't buy more." Next the buddhi eliminated three chocolate bars as inferior, but was still confused about how to choose among the other fifteen. Impelled by the craving for chocolate, but unable to make a clear decision, the buddhi motivated Fred to grab four chocolate bars at random. Fred filed this information in his memory-field as "chocolate samskara 4" with a note identifying the four bars he actually ended up buying.

Add all these up and we can see that Fred has collected seventy-seven chocolate samskaras, although he bought only four varieties. The first twenty samskaras, engendered at the sensory level, are quite vague. The samskaras related to the four varieties he bought are the strongest, but they contain the awareness of confusion and randomness. The samskaras in between get gradually stronger, but are devoid of the samskara of purpose.

Now let's imagine an attorney—we'll call her Elaine—who has completed her duties in a peaceful frame of mind. She too hears that there is a storm on the way and decides to stop at the grocery store on the way home to buy her favorite chocolate. She walks purposefully to the candy section. At the sensory level she notices the twenty different kinds of chocolate bars on display, but she is so clear about what she wants that she barely perceives nineteen of them. She identifies the one she came for, takes it from the shelf, and walks directly back to the checkout counter.

In her case too there are impressions of twenty varieties of chocolate stored as "chocolate samskara 1," but they are so vague and weak that they hardly occupy any space in her memory-field. Versions 2 and 3 contain only one chocolate, and they too occupy almost no space in her memory. "Chocolate samskara 4" contains one strong, clear impression, and it is filed so distinctly that Elaine can retrieve it at any time almost without effort. Thus she has created only twenty-three chocolate samskaras, twenty-two of which have no power to motivate her to buy chocolate in the future. The twenty-third is endowed with clarity and purpose, but it can motivate her only if she wishes it. Fred's mind, on the other hand, will be tossed about by the confusing chocolate samskaras he has created, and he has no choice but to behave like a slave to them.

This example may seem frivolous, but it explains how we create samskaras. If Fred's mind is bogged down by all the virtually useless chocolate samskaras he created in the space of a few minutes, think of the numberless samskaras we fill our minds with in the long journey of life. The more unstable the mind and the more sensory objects it contacts, the more samskaras are created and stored. And when actions are accompanied by confusion in the first place, their corresponding samskaras are imbued with confusion. Memories related to these samskaras in turn inspire the conscious mind and senses to undertake similar confused actions.

Fred's problem apparently began when he got the telephone calls from his client and the children's school; it deepened when he talked to his wife, and got even worse when the children demanded computer games: this chain of events disturbed his equilibrium. According to yoga psychology, Fred's rajas became agitated when his equilibrium was disturbed; sattva and tamas immediately declined sharply. If Fred had had a sattvic temperament, he would have maintained his equilibrium in spite of all these external circumstances, for if sattva is dominant, rajas will be held in check and cannot rise above a certain level.

It is often assumed that loss of equilibrium is triggered at the level of our biochemistry. In other words, external circumstances cause our adrenaline levels to rise, and that leads us to become agitated. Yet some people do not experience an adrenaline rush in the same situations that disturb others. It is not the external situation nor the adrenaline that disturbs our equilibrium, but the interplay of sattva, rajas, and tamas and the dominance of one over the others. People dominated by sattvic energy are composed, those dominated by rajasic energy are agitated, and those dominated by tamasic energy are depressed.

Getting Clear

If we want to make sure that our mind functions in a balanced way, we must first increase the level of sattva and let rajas and tamas become subordinate. Under the influence of sattvic energy we can think clearly, make the right decisions, and summon our will and determination. This will engender positive karmas and prevent negative ones from forming. But it requires creating an environment which attracts sattvic energies from every direction and repels rajasic and tamasic ones. To do this we have to be vigilant in all areas of our life: how we sleep, what we eat, what we read, how we exercise, and how we interact with others. In short, we have to bring a sattvic quality to all our actions—physical, verbal, and mental.

In the area of diet, for example, we must eat sattvic food and avoid rajasic and tamasic food. Sattvic food is light, fresh, easily digestible, nutritious, and neither overcooked nor undercooked. Rajasic food has a strong taste; it is heavily spiced, fiery, salty; it aggravates our digestive system, disturbs our sleep, and causes unpleasant dreams. Tamasic food is stale, heavy, overcooked, and composed of so many ingredients that it is hard to identify the main one; it is loaded with additives and preservatives, and may be overly sweet; it is hard to digest, and makes us slothful and sleepy.

How we entertain ourselves also has a strong bearing on our temperament. Entertainment that delights the senses while leaving them calm, has a tranquil effect on the mind, does not linger in the mind afterwards, and is spiritually inspiring is sattvic. Rajasic entertainment is exciting; it is associated with loud sounds, bright lights and colors; it is fast-moving, violent, romantic, or tragic—it agitates our emotions. Entertainment that is dull, boring, and leads to inertia is tamasic.

If we pay attention to these and other areas of our life with a view to increasing our sattvic energies, we can make our mind balanced, focused, sharp, and penetrating. A balanced, sattvic mind then has the capacity to withstand the internal turmoil caused by the rajasic and tamasic effects of our dormant and active karmas. Although our efforts to increase sattvic energy do not destroy these karmas, if we adopt a sattvic lifestyle the tamasic and rajasic effects of these karmas will be neutralized significantly.

A sattvic mind is free from attachment, anger, desire, hatred, jealousy, greed, and ego. Because the mind is more subtle than the body and senses, a sattvic mind will send waves of sattvic energy into the body and senses, and they will lose their rajasic and tamasic cravings. Even the primitive urges of hunger, sleep, sex, and self-preservation will be sattvic, thereby causing little turmoil in our life. What is more, increasing our sattvic energy will significantly reduce our confusion.

Patanjali, the author of the *Yoga Sutra,* and Vyasa, its foremost commentator, tell us that a confused mind is not fit to follow the path of yoga. Such a mind is dominated by tamas and rajas and fails to envision the highest good, so it has little inclination to perform those actions which have the highest good as their goal. Even if it does perform such actions, it generates so much confusion that the subtle impressions stored in the form of dormant karma are totally contaminated. In short, although auspicious actions performed by a confused person will create karmas conducive to spiritual growth, they will not be altogether free of negative effects. Preparatory practices, however, can purify and discipline the mind so that it no longer shifts among disturbed, distracted, and stupefied states.

This does not mean that we should not attempt to do anything good until we have attained complete freedom from confusion. It is true that our present and future actions are primarily motivated by our destiny—our prarabdha karmas—and in relation to those karmas we have virtually no freedom of choice. But the main prarabdha karma is always accompanied by a host of secondary karmic strands, and in relation to these we have greater freedom to make choices.

To clarify the relationship between the central and secondary strands of prarabdha karma, let's return to the story of the brahmin and his beloved horse. It was his destiny to have one horse. Honoring the advice of sage Narada, the brahmin overcame his attachment to that horse by summoning his power of will and determination, and getting rid of it. By doing so he manipulated his secondary karmas, which were causing his wife to spend her days getting food for the horse and were forcing him to look for students for his livelihood rather than as a form of service.

Another story, this one from the *Srimad Bhagavatam,* will further clarify the relationship between the main and secondary karmic strands of our destiny. It will show how our present actions can influence our secondary active karmas.

———

Shortly before Lord Krishna was born in the lineage of King Yadu, a young sage named Gargya was wed to a princess in that lineage. They lived together happily in Mathura, the capital city, until, with the consent of his wife, the sage undertook an intense spiritual practice which required that he eat very little and practice celibacy. He had explained the nature of the practice to his wife, but she did not realize he would be so adamant about following it. As time went on, she began to feel abandoned and depressed, and finally expressed her unhappiness to her brothers.

Because of his restricted diet the sage had become thin and looked quite weak. It was rumored that he was impotent and was using the practice to hide his problem. So the princess' brothers, probably driven by their active karmas, began to harass and abuse him. The sage remained calm and tranquil for a long time, but the harassment continued unabated. At last he lost his temper. "How potent I am will become apparent when my son is born," he said. "My son will be invincible to the entire Yadu clan, and even Lord Narayana, who will soon incarnate in that clan in the form of Krishna, will not be able to defeat him."

So saying, the sage abandoned Mathura and moved westward. He traveled all the way to what is now Turkey and settled there, and after a few years he had a son with a woman from a family of cowherds. Soon after the child was born, the sage returned to his homeland and rededicated his life to his spiritual practice. Meanwhile his son, Kalayavana, grew up to be a great warrior. He conquered the region east of Turkey and expanded his empire all the way to the western border of India, where several Indian kings became his friends.

In the interim, Lord Krishna had been born in Mathura in the lineage of King Yadu and grew to be an unmatched warrior. But for political reasons many Indian kings turned against him, joining together to consolidate their power. They asked Kalayavana to come to their aid. Kalayavana had no personal reason to consider Krishna his enemy. In fact, Krishna had always treated him as a friend and relative, and because they were both in the lineage of King Yadu, Kalayavana had reason to ally himself with Krishna. But his friendship with the Indian kings who were Krishna's enemies, and the knowledge that Krishna's relatives had taunted his father, persuaded Kalayavana to turn against Krishna and take revenge for his father's humiliation. Besides, he knew that he could not be defeated by anyone belonging to the lineage of King Yadu. So Kalayavana joined forces with Krishna's enemies and attacked Mathura.

Krishna, who was omniscient and almighty, knew he could not defeat Kalayavana without violating the law of destiny— and so, at the cost of great destruction, pain, and dishonor, he fled from the battlefield. The invincible Kalayavana gave chase and attempted to capture him. Like a coward, Krishna kept running, Kalayavana at his heels. After several days, Krishna darted into a large cave. A man was sleeping there in the darkness. Krishna threw his shawl over the sleeper and hid himself at the back of the cave. In a few minutes, Kalayavana rushed in. Recognizing Krishna's golden shawl, he kicked the sleeper. The instant the man woke up, flames shot from his eyes, incinerating Kalayavana. In this way Krishna's enemy was destroyed, but the law of destiny was upheld.

Before we attempt to analyze the law of destiny and its relationship with secondary karmas, let us see who the sleeping man was. Several thousand years earlier, in the *satya yuga,* this man was known as King Muchukunda—a noble king, a valiant warrior, and an accomplished yogi. King Muchukunda ruled a land bordered by the Himalayas in the north and the ocean in three other directions, and while he was living in the world his consciousness merged in Bhagavan Narayana. For several hundred years he worked day and night to bring both external prosperity and internal happiness to his empire. He stamped out the forces of destruction and negativity, and there was peace and prosperity everywhere. Hatred and greed vanished from his kingdom. Even the celestial beings longed to be born in the land he ruled.

Indra, the king of divine beings, visited King Muchukunda one day, and to honor him he told the king to ask for a boon. The king replied, "If my kingdom is safe and my time for serving it is over, please grant me a long rest." So Indra taught him the technique of preserving his body while he went into *yoga nidra* (yogic sleep) and showed him a cave where he could rest undisturbed. Indra also decreed that if anyone should awaken him forcibly, that person would be reduced to ashes through his yogic fire. So the adept went into sleepless sleep with his consciousness fully absorbed in Bhagavan Narayana.

When Kalayavana awakened the yogi with a kick and was consequently reduced to ashes, Krishna emerged from the back of the cave, shining in his full glory. King Muchukunda could not believe his eyes: here was the highest form of beauty and bliss, standing personified in front of him. His whole being was pervaded by indescribable, supernal joy. Realizing that Krishna was none other than the Lord of Life, he prostrated himself at Krishna's feet, where he received the highest grace. Then, guided by Krishna, he retreated into the deep Himalayas, where he took *mahasamadhi,* leaving his body in the most exalted yogic manner.

In this story, the main strand of Kalayavana's destiny ensured that he would not be defeated or killed by anybody from the lineage of King Yadu, including Krishna. His secondary karmas caused him to have Krishna's enemies as his friends and engendered the desire to avenge his father. Muchukunda's main active karma dictated that he would see his Lord face to face. Krishna, on the other hand, was free from all karmas and was motivated only by his own intrinsic wisdom and compassion.

Kalayavana could have chosen to deal with his friends wisely; he was free to do so. By themselves the secondary karma of friendship with Krishna's enemies was not strong enough to invite animosity toward Krishna. But this secondary karma in combination with another—his desire to avenge the insult to his father—tipped the scales and inspired him to take up arms against Krishna, which created a new field of potential karmas. Potential karmas immediately turn into dormant karmas and later manifest as powerful active karmas.

By embracing the spiritual disciplines of love, compassion, forgiveness, and nonattachment—and, what is more important, by using his own power of will and determination— Kalayavana could have avoided the fight with Krishna. But he had neglected the spiritual virtues, and this neglect supported his secondary karmas in creating a new set of potential karmas. These potential karmas, combined with the dormant karmas already stored, supported the main strands of his destiny, and vice versa. Eventually Kalayavana became so entangled in this web that he could not extricate himself. As a result his life came to an end.

Similarly, Muchukunda's main destiny was to come face to face with Krishna, not incinerating Kalayavana. Had he been dominated by rajas he would have become so enraged at being awakened with a kick that he would have ignored Krishna, but because he was established in the higher virtues of nonattachment, forgiveness, and compassion, his mind did not linger on the person who woke him up. Because he paid hardly any attention to Kalayavana, he did not allow any of his secondary karmas to influence him adversely.

Creating Positive Karmas

We can summon our power of will and determination to make a decision and act on that decision, even if secondary karmas stored in the past are exerting an influence on us in the present. It is entirely up to us to create potential karmas that are conducive to our growth. If we decide to make an effort to perform sattvic actions, such actions will engender sattvic fruits, helping us to purify our mind and minimize confusion. There is nothing in our destiny that we ourselves did not create. The results of actions we performed long ago have manifested as our current destiny, just as the actions we are performing today will manifest as our future destiny. Even if we have a confused mind, we must make an effort to perform actions which are conducive to our well-being. We must never forget that as humans we have a great degree of freedom of choice. With effort we can focus our scattered mind momentarily and make a decision to involve ourselves only in wholesome actions. We may not always succeed, but we can keep trying.

Committing ourselves to such a course of action and staying with it for a prolonged period is called spiritual practice. The scriptures tell us that it is the practice that makes us perfect—by undertaking positive actions we create positive potential karmas, which serve as an antidote to the karmas that have caused our mind to become scattered. These positive potential karmas will be deposited in the unconscious mind in a dormant form; later they will influence our present and future actions. That is why we must attend to our present actions and refrain from blaming our karmas for our confusion and scatteredness. According to yoga, we can incorporate three spiritual practices into our lives which will do much to loosen the grip of our negative karmas: cultivating focus, exercising control over our senses, and strengthening our power of will and determination.

Forming a habit of staying focused will prevent us from involving ourselves in useless actions. Like children, we are often more interested in knowing what others are doing than in doing what we need to do. This leads us to compare ourselves with others and engenders inferiority and superiority complexes, creating an environment in which hatred, jealousy, greed, and competitiveness flourish. Such feelings pollute our mind and force us to involve ourselves in unnecessary actions. By performing unnecessary actions we create unnecessary karmas, which perpetuate our confusion and complicate our life.

The next step is to practice *pratyahara* (sense withdrawal). The mind cannot execute its plans without the help of the senses. A sattvic mind employs them to complete its chosen tasks. When tamas is dominant, however, the mind becomes careless and begins to depend on the senses. The senses take advantage of this dependency—their cravings grow into urges, and these urges draw the mind toward pleasurable objects. Eventually the mind becomes subservient to the senses. This is a recipe for a scattered mind—the senses are constantly employing the mind to contact, perceive, feel, and judge the pleasure and pain contained in sensory objects. And we perform our actions under the influence of these sensory urges, creating potential karmas contaminated by craving and confusion.

The senses are many and powerful. By offering us a modicum of what seems to be pleasure, the senses of taste, touch, smell, sight, and hearing compel the mind to run from one object to another. They promise great fulfillment, and the mind believes them. But soon after the mind embraces an object, it is disappointed—the joy of this embrace was not as profound and long-lasting as it had hoped. Through its own experience, the mind knows that sensory pleasures have no real value, yet under the sway of the senses it allows itself to be attracted by the charms and temptations of objects again and again, only to encounter repeated disappointment. Realizing its folly, the mind often decides not to waste time in such acts, but, driven by sensory urges, it fails to act on this decision. Eventually the mind becomes frustrated and loses its self-confidence and self-respect. From that point on, it continues performing actions without knowing why.

Freeing ourselves from this cycle requires disciplining the senses. The scriptures tell us that "discipline which has provision for training and taming the senses alone qualifies as yoga practice. Only by undertaking such a yoga practice can one prevent oneself from falling into the trap of negligence and self-deception. Such practice alone enables an aspirant to break the cycle of birth and death." (*Katha Upanishad* 2:3:11)

In other words, to extricate the mind from this endless cycle we must work with our senses. But it is impossible to begin with all of them simultaneously, especially when they have come to dominate the mind. We must choose one and concentrate on bringing it under control.

In the Bhagavad Gita, Lord Krishna advises us to begin by working with the tongue, the abode of two senses—taste and speech—because the influence of taste supersedes all other urges and motivates many of our actions. Even though taste is generally associated with food, in truth anything we take in has a taste. The taste buds on our tongue experience pleasure related to food, but the experiences corresponding to the other sense organs are ultimately savored by the mind—and those experiences are expressed through our tongue in the form of speech. Words rolling off our tongue are the manifestation of our thoughts, which themselves are generated in response to our sensory perceptions and feelings. Whether or not we express them aloud, we cannot comprehend our own thoughts and feelings without putting them into words. In short, we cannot think without words, and words are expressed aloud through the tongue.

Thus at some point any experience of sense pleasure is related to the tongue, and one means of disciplining the senses is to discipline the tongue by regulating both our diet and our speech. When these are regulated properly, our actions are better organized and our life becomes less complicated. A simple life provides fewer opportunities for the mind to be confused and scattered. And with a more organized and peaceful mind we can perform actions that create positive karmas.

The third and most important action we can undertake to overcome the confusion in our mind is to build our *sankalpa shakti* (the power of will and determination). The same mind that has the capacity to create karmas in the first place (and to be influenced later by its own karmic accumulations) also has the power to dismantle previous karmas and rebuild according to a well-thought-out plan.

Ordinarily we surrender ourselves to the force of karma because we are not aware of the power of the mind. But according to *jnana* yoga (the yoga of knowledge) karmas are created, sustained, and executed by the magical power of the mind. Getting caught in the net of our karmas is like a magician becoming mesmerized by his own magic. In other words, the mind is the cause of both bondage and liberation. The key to unlocking the mind's liberating power is *sankalpa shakti;* the failure to use this power of will and determination is the source of misery. As humans, we have the capacity to overcome our self-created karmic misery, provided we unfold our *sankalpa shakti* to its fullest. As the following story from the Puranas shows, even those with a great deal of self-knowledge create long-lasting misery for themselves if they do not employ their power of will and determination.

Rama was the ideal king, tending to the needs of his subjects in matters both great and small. One day he asked his brother, Lakshmana, to see if there was anyone in the palace courtyard seeking an audience with the king. Lakshmana went out and looked around, but saw nothing out of the ordinary. Rama, however, was not satisfied with this and asked Lakshmana to look once more.

Again Lakshmana went outside and stood on the palace steps, but saw no one who seemed anxious or unhappy. Then, as he stood there puzzled, he noticed a dejected-looking dog and saw that it had been wounded in the head. When Lakshmana came nearer, the dog stood up and began to cry. In those days, rulers and those in high positions had the ability to understand the language of other creatures, so Lakshmana addressed the dog, asking about the cause of his tears. The dog bowed his head and said he wanted justice from Rama, so Lakshmana took him to the king.

Assembling his counselors, Rama invited the dog to speak openly and without fear. "Your majesty, you are our protector and the provider of justice," the dog began. "A beggar named Sarvartha Siddha hit me on the head for no reason. I pray that you will grant me justice."

Sarvartha Siddha was summoned immediately and invited to present his side of the story. Without hesitation the man confessed. "Lord, it is true that I struck this dog out of anger. It happened as I was on my way to ask for alms. I had been walking for hours and I was overcome by hunger. This animal was sitting on a narrow trail. When I asked him to move so I could pass, he didn't budge. I lost my temper and struck him on the head. I am at fault; I deserve punishment."

Turning to his advisers, Rama asked them to assign an appropriate punishment. But, after conferring for a few moments, they replied, "This is a complicated case, involving as it does a human being and an animal. In addition, this beggar is a brahmin, so he cannot be punished in any way that entails physical pain. We are at a loss to know what punishment to give, but this dog has sought refuge in your protection, and you must provide it."

Rama turned to the dog and asked if he had anything to say. "Yes, your majesty," the dog replied. "With your permission, I will offer a solution to the problem: appoint him the head of the monastery at Kalinger."

To everyone's amazement, Rama agreed. The beggar, delighted with this punishment, mounted an elephant provided by Rama and left to assume his new post. To the bewildered counselors, it seemed as if the beggar had been rewarded for his misdeeds. When they said as much to Rama, the king asked the dog to unravel the mystery and explain why granting the beggar the post of head monk at the Kalinger monastery was a form of punishment.

Without a moment's hesitation the dog replied, "I will explain, your majesty. In my previous lifetime I was the head of that monastery. I got this appointment because I was born into a learned and prestigious family. I had studied the scriptures and had a strong desire to use my position for my own spiritual fulfillment as well as that of the monks and of the people the monastery served. During my long tenure I took good care of those who worked under me. I worshiped God sincerely. Yet in spite of these good acts I have been reborn a dog.

"It happened because I did not pay attention to the subtle mental impressions which caused me to find pleasure in name and fame—even though I also had a strong desire for liberation. Because of my position, people treated me as a holy man, and I too came to believe that I was holy. But deep in my heart I knew that my position had not completely transformed me. Yet for the sake of prestige, I pretended that it had. When I assumed my post, my desire for the ultimate spiritual knowledge was quite powerful. Had I focused my willpower on achieving that goal at all costs, the transformation I was seeking would surely have come about. But I did not remain focused.

"Faithful followers trusted me to be selfless. They offered me donations for religious and charitable purposes, and I accepted them in the name of God. But because I was lacking in self-analysis and introspection, I began, as time passed, to use some of this money for my own comfort. Each time I did so my conscience told me that I was committing a mistake, but my mind justified my act. 'A person in my position needs to be impressive,' I told myself. 'My prestige and the prestige of the Kalinger monastery are one and the same.' My conscience contradicted these justifications, but I did not heed it.

"Finally, failure to heed the voice of conscience damaged my willpower so badly that in spite of knowing what was right and what was wrong—which actions would lead to further bondage and which to liberation—I could not control my actions. Instead of governing my life through the power of will and determination, the charms and temptations of the world gradually became my governing force. And in time my willpower became so weak that I no longer had the courage to even acknowledge the battle between my tricky mind and my conscience. The desire for liberation gave way to the desire for a comfortable life. I began eating sumptuous food, wearing splendid ornaments and vestments, and indulging in all manner of luxuries."

The dog paused for a moment, and then concluded: "The beggar who attacked me is angry and violent and has no control over his senses and appetites. As head of that monastery, he will fall into the same trap I fell into. His own karmas will punish him, just as mine have punished me."

This story illustrates the crucial role of *sankalpa shakti* in either unfolding or suppressing the intrinsic powers of the mind to liberate itself. According to the sage Vyasa, the mind is imbued with seven such intrinsic powers. They are:

Shakti—the power to be and the power to become. This is the fundamental force necessary to accomplish any task.

Cheshta—purposeful movement.

Jivana—the capacity to contain the life-force and thus to keep an organism alive.

Parinama—the capacity to keep changing from one state to another, from one mood to another.

Nirodha—the capacity to stop shifting from one state to another. This is the mind's capacity to control and rescue itself even when it seems to be totally disorganized and lost.

Samskara—the capacity to store the subtle impression of an action, or any information the mind gathers from any source.

Dharma—the power that naturally inclines the mind toward freedom and inner fulfillment.

Due to a lack of spiritual training we usually experience only the functioning of the sixth force, *samskara*, but because we also have the other six intrinsic capacities, there is always a way to accomplish our goal. Regardless of the state of our mind—how confused or clear it is, how disturbed or composed, how dull or vibrant, inspired or depressed—we can meet the challenge of any problem, provided we have access to these intrinsic forces. Spiritual training provides this access.

Success in any endeavor—spiritual or worldly—comes from cultivating the conviction that we have the power to accomplish anything, the power to be and become whatever we want. This conviction introduces us to the mind's first intrinsic capacity, *shakti,* which is the key to attaining mastery over the other six. As the story shows, *shakti* plays the pivotal role in the unfolding or suppressing of the other six characteristics. The dog, in his earlier life as head of the monastery, was at first aware of the subtle functioning of his mind. As he became careless and the charms and temptations of the world began to enslave him, he started to lose mastery over his mind. Failure to exercise his willpower and determination caused him to become weak, and the subtle impressions of his past actions then influenced his present actions. Due to his declining willpower and weakening determination he lost control over *dharma,* the power that makes the mind naturally inclined toward freedom and inner fulfillment. Gradually his life came to be governed only by *samskara,* through which the mind stores the impressions of our deeds. Had the chief monk awakened the force of *sankalpa shakti* he could have channeled the powers of *cheshta, parinama, nirodha,* and *samskara* to awaken *dharma.* And by doing so, his desire for liberation would have been strengthened and his tendency to misappropriate that which had been offered to God would have been extinguished.

Due to lack of spiritual awareness, however, most of us experience only the functioning of *samskara,* through which the mind continuously stores the subtle impressions of our actions. This storage space, called the unconscious mind, is expanded in the process. *Jivana* gives life to all the stored contents. It keeps the past alive in the form of *samskaras,* and *cheshta* stirs these subtle impressions, giving them momentum to manifest. Thus it is the mind's own power that awakens the stored karmas, transforming them into the active karmas that constitute our destiny.

The storage space of our karmas, the unconscious mind, is also a creation of the mind. And once it is fully formed, our decision-making faculty is heavily influenced by the powerful subtle impressions stored there. That is why even though we know what is right at a conscious level, we are not motivated to do it; that is also why we fail to stop doing that which we know is harmful. Our personality traits, in turn, evolve along the pattern established by the contents of our unconscious mind and shape our tastes, interests, and choices. To discover why this is so, and to continue adding to our knowledge of how to attain freedom from the wheel of karma, we must embark on a study of the unconscious mind and its relationship with the conscious mind.

Chapter Four

The Weaver of Destiny

ACCORDING TO YOGA, the mind has two aspects: conscious, and unconscious. The conscious mind works during our waking state and is always accompanied by the senses. It is the part of the mind that uses the brain as its seat and functions in response to sense stimuli. This mind is called *manas*. The totality of the mind (which includes manas as well as the vast unconscious) is known as *chitta*. Using the senses as its instruments, manas gathers data related to external objects and, through further processing, perceives them distinctly, identifies them as good or bad, and decides to respond to them positively or negatively. The conscious mind stores information at each step, some in the conscious memory, and some in the unconscious. This process was illustrated by the story of Fred and his chocolate in the previous chapter.

The unconscious mind is where our mental experiences are stored in the form of subtle impressions (samskaras); it is called unconscious because we are not ordinarily aware of its existence, let alone of the contents deposited there. In other words, we do not have conscious access to this aspect of the mind.

The relationship between the conscious and unconscious mind is like that of a house and its basement: the basement is the unconscious mind, and the rest of the house is the conscious mind. Some of us keep our basement clean, well lighted, and properly organized. We maintain an accurate inventory of what we have stored there, and from time to time we retrieve items that we need. Others of us rarely visit our basement. We just toss stuff in and forget about it, letting everything accumulate in a jumble.

The rooms we live in can be compared to the conscious mind, which employs the five senses and entertains itself with the objects of the world. The conscious mind also gathers information and provides training to itself as well as to the senses and other aspects of our personality.

When we buy a house we purchase furniture, rugs, lamps, and other things we need, and then we arrange them properly. We go shopping from time to time and acquire more items for the house—a new sofa, another carpet, a better dining room table—and we put old ones in the basement. As time passes, the basement gradually fills up. We still find ourselves attracted to new items, but since the basement is full and the rest of the house is completely furnished, we rearrange the already existing furnishings to accommodate the new ones. Eventually the rooms become crowded and all the closets, cupboards, and shelves are crammed. Next we start stuffing things under couches and counters and making piles in corners and against the walls, until there is hardly any space left anywhere.

Our living quarters, which were once spacious, are now cluttered and cramped, and it is almost impossible to move around without bumping into a jumble of one thing or another. The whole house has become so congested and disorganized that we rarely find what we are looking for, and if the need for something we can't find is pressing enough, we simply go out and buy another of its kind.

Our mind is like that. When the human race was young there was a time when we were fully aware of all the mind's contents—both conscious and unconscious. The storage space was small and easily accessible; we knew exactly what was kept there, and where everything was. But as we started accumulating the impressions of objects and experiences, we needed more and more storage space. With every successive lifetime we have more and more stored items from the past, so as the deepest recesses of our original storage space have become filled, we have turned other areas of our mind into storage space. And just as living area shrinks as more and more of the house is converted to storage, part of the mind which was at one time fully conscious, clean, and transparent has become unconscious, congested, and opaque.

The size of the brain and the trillions of neurons it contains indicates that it is possible for an incredible amount of knowledge to be at the disposal of the conscious mind. At one time people had ready access to this information because they had a greater degree of retentive power than we do today and they were able to retrieve information more efficiently than we can. At that time, many people had access to the past and future, not just prophets and sages. We see this in the stories found in Vedic and Puranic literature as well as in the Old Testament, where we read about people who could communicate with animals and plants.

Nature provided us with an organized brain so we can process, assimilate, and retrieve information. Today, however, our minds are overloaded, and what is more, with the advent

of calculators, computers, and fast-moving images, our attention span is shrinking rapidly. Less than five percent of our
brain is active; the rest is dormant. We are using the conscious
mind less and dumping more information into an already congested unconscious.

As a result, most of our activities are governed by the
unconscious mind. For instance, we know that commercials
and advertisements rarely present the complete truth, yet we
are heavily influenced by them. Messages from cigarette and
liquor advertisements, for example, have been deeply im-
planted in our unconscious mind, and as a result the tiny
part of the conscious mind that knows how damaging they
are to our health is not always able to stop many of us from
using those substances. In large measure, we are slaves of our
unconscious.

Our modern system of education trains only the conscious
part of our mind, and that training does not include training
us in how to use the conscious mind to gain freedom from
our slavery to the unconscious mind. No one teaches us how
to cleanse the unconscious, or how to expand the space in
the conscious realm, or—the most crucial skill of all—how to
penetrate the unconscious consciously. If we could do that,
if we could enter the unconscious mind consciously and take
an inventory of the contents deposited there, we could design
an effective and realistic system for inner transformation. This
skill can be cultivated through meditation. With it, we can
precisely target and attenuate the negative impressions stored
in the unconscious and strengthen the positive ones, and this
speeds up our inner journey.

As it is, however, we have neither the knowledge nor the
ability to open the door of our unconscious mind. The base-

ment has been locked and ignored for so long that we have forgotten what it looks like, and we have no idea of what is hidden there. Thus it is impossible to formulate a plan for organizing the contents of our basement and getting rid of the junk.

The deeper the unconscious contents of our mind are buried, and the more densely they are packed into the storage place, the more likely they are to explode, shaking the entire structure so violently that the weak parts shatter. We feel the blast, but because we do not know what exploded or why, we call the trauma destiny, God's will, or an accident. And even if our karmic bombs do not actually explode, they create constant tremors, making us insecure, anxious, and fearful. Most of our conscious activities are influenced by this precarious state.

We perform most of our actions either to achieve that which we do not yet have or to preserve that which we do have. Actions performed under these conditions are motivated by the unconscious; what seems to be our immediate motive in the conscious realm is in reality only the catalyst for activating samskaras in the unconscious. It is the samskara that motivates the conscious mind to employ the body and sensory organs to perform an action. To illustrate this point, let's consider a story from the *Srimad Bhagavatam*.

———

Once upon a time there was a sage named Saubhari who lived in solitude. For many years he dedicated himself totally to the practice of austerities and meditation, and by the time he reached a ripe old age everyone in the kingdom knew him. Merchants, philosophers, and even the royal family respected him.

One day Saubhari went to bathe in a nearby lake, and

remained in the water to do his special twilight meditation. As he opened his eyes to fill his palms with water, he noticed a school of small fish frolicking with their mother. They seemed to be having such fun that the sage used his extraordinary intuitive power to understand why they were so happy—and he was surprised to realize the profound joy the mother felt at being the parent of so many delightful young ones. "The fish in the lake are so joyful," the sage thought. "I have spent my whole life doing spiritual practices, and I have not experienced this. I too should have children. I must get married." With this thought he came out of the lake and began formulating a plan.

After making inquiries, the sage learned that the king had fifty daughters, all of whom were of marriageable age, so he decided to pay him a visit. When the king heard that Saubhari had come to see him, he greeted him with great respect and asked how he could serve him. The holy man replied frankly that he wanted to get married and had heard that the king's daughters were of marriageable age.

Although the king had great reverence for the sage, he could not bring himself to give any of his daughters in marriage to such an old man. But at the same time, he could not refuse him bluntly. So, humbly and diplomatically he said that since his daughters were grown, it would be better if their feelings were honored. If any of them agreed to marry the sage, the king would give his consent. The sage understood what the king meant, so using his wisdom and yogic power, he rejuvenated himself and reversed his age, transforming himself into a handsome young man.

When he met the princesses, one after the other, all agreed to marry him, so he wed all fifty and brought them to his ashram. There he lived the life of a householder, and had a hundred children, two with each wife.

———

This simple story tells us a lot about the effects of the unconscious on our conscious decision-making. Watching the school of fish swimming happily around their mother was not the main motivating force behind the sage's decision to get married. That incident simply revived memories—the subtle impressions of being married and having children—that were buried deep in his unconscious. The sight was like a pebble thrown into a lake: the ripples kept spreading outward until they reached the shore of the sage's conscious mind. In the same way, stimulated by external events, our samskaras are awakened and create ripples deep in our unconscious. These ripples spread outward, influencing our conscious mind, which in turn motivates our senses, our brain, and the rest of our limbs and organs to undertake an action.

As we have seen, there are numberless dormant karmas stored in the unconscious. Some are powerful, others relatively weak; some are central, others secondary. Generally speaking, the main karmas are accompanied by a number of secondary karmas. Only one karma or group of karmas awakens at a time, and when it does, it influences our conscious mind in a specific manner.

It is not easy to pinpoint what exactly determines which particular karma or group of karmas will dictate our behavior, and when. The scriptures constantly remind us that only the omniscient Divine Being understands the precise dynamics of karma and its relationship to the cycle of birth and death. However, the scriptures do spell out what the sages in the past have confirmed through their intuitive wisdom: the grand plan of destiny—our prarabdha karma—is set before the beginning of each lifetime. Under normal circumstances it cannot be changed or even modified. For example, the kind of body we are born in, how long we will live in that body, and whether we will be basically happy or unhappy during that lifetime is determined by destiny before we are born.

In general, the law of karma holds that with every action we create a subtle impression, which is then stored in the unconscious as a samskara. Under normal circumstances every impression will eventually ripen and manifest in the form of destiny. Powerful impressions individually or collectively become the main strands of our destiny; other impressions coalesce around them in the form of secondary karmas. The main strands dictate which body we will be born into, how long we will live, and whether the experience we undergo during that lifetime will be pleasant or unpleasant. The secondary karmas fill in the details. Although we cannot change the course of our main destiny, we have some degree of choice in manipulating our secondary karmas, and thereby, to some extent, we can influence our destiny.

The main active karma is like a blueprint for a house. The secondary dormant karmas and the secondary strands of destiny provide the details. The blueprint determines the basic shape and structure and cannot be modified. Secondary karmas are like the finishing materials and decorative details that complete the house. As the construction progresses, the architect has nothing to say about where, when, and how we hang curtains or paintings, what color we paint our shutters, or how we arrange our furniture. These are like secondary karmas.

The trivial, day-to-day details—losing something and getting something else, how we spend our time on a particular weekend—are secondary karmas that revolve around the main strand of destiny. For example, the sage's marriage to fifty princesses was part of his main destiny. The overall quality of his life after he got married was also part of his central karma. But the size of the houses he built for each wife and her children, how he divided his attention among them, and how he managed his daily spiritual practices in such a complex household were the result of his secondary karmas. Here he had a great deal of flexibility in his choices. Once married, he was at a crossroads—either he could drown in the circumstances which usually emerge once a man starts living with more than one woman, or he could maintain his inner wisdom and live in the world while remaining above it. To us, it seems impossible to relate to fifty wives, raise a hundred children, and attend to the worldly details associated with a family of this size. But the sage did not allow any of his secondary karmas to affect the central karmic strand of his destiny in an adverse manner. He continued his spiritual practice as one-pointedly as before, kept all his wives happy, and raised his children, many of whom turned out to be great rulers and spiritual adepts.

The sage was wise, spiritually powerful, and skillful in a worldly sense. These qualities are underdeveloped in most of us—we struggle from inner poverty and lack of skill in managing our affairs. We are like homeowners who must use old and leftover materials to renovate our homes even if they do not serve our purpose. We don't have the knowledge, the resources, or the ability to acquire the best available materials and use them in a suitable manner. Furthermore, we are attached to what we have already accumulated and want to keep it whether or not we have a use for it. By the same token, because of our lack of knowledge and dispassion we fail to exercise our power of will and determination in choosing, accepting, and discarding our secondary karmas.

Therefore the answer to the question "What determines which particular karma or group of karmas will dictate our behavior, and when?" is both simple and complex. The simple part of the answer is that destiny in the form of active karmas has its own course, and we have no power to change it. The complex part of the answer involves an explanation of secondary karmas—how they gather around the main karmic strands of destiny, and how they dictate our behavior. Some secondary karmas can be manipulated, but if they are strong and are deeply entwined with the main karma it is almost impossible to prevent them from manifesting or to modify their effect after they have manifested. Or even if they are not deeply entwined with the main karma, they can be like tentacles radiating from it and connecting one person's destiny with another's, thus opening a channel between personal karma and group karma. Only the knowers of destiny can see precisely how these tentacles of secondary karmas are connected to the tentacles radiating from the main destiny of others. In very rare cases, such accomplished masters can cut the tentacles of destiny, and thereby disconnect one person's fate from the fate of others. Or, if necessary, they can connect one person's fate with another's fate or with the fate of others by intertwining secondary karmas.

I came to understand this when I was fortunate enough to watch a saint working with the secondary karmas of a young man who was born with a heart defect. Although this young man had undergone valve-replacement surgery in his childhood, he was never very strong and had to be extremely careful with his health. His mother was deeply attached to him, her only son, and they both revered the saint and visited him regularly. For reasons unknown to me, the saint was constantly urging the young man to get married. One day when I felt that the saint was in the mood to explain the subtle mysteries of life, I asked him what he was trying to accomplish by encouraging the young man to get married. He explained that since this young man had long-standing health problems, he might not live long unless something drastic was done. When I asked about further medical treatment, the saint said the young man had already undergone the best possible treatments and that changes now had to be made in the realm of his fate.

Here is how the saint described the karmic conditions prevailing in that sickly young man: His mother was very much attached to him; the two were karmically connected, and it was her destiny to lose her son. If she disowned him or if she renounced her relationship with him, his health would improve. But that was not an option, because neither mother nor son was ready to understand this subtle point.

The other option was for him to get married—marriage binds two people's destinies together. If he married a woman whose destiny was to have a long-lasting marital relationship with a healthy husband, this young man's destiny would be modified. He was currently attracted to a young woman whose family was close to his mother's relatives. Once married, the couple would live near the young man's mother—so that by marrying that woman he would reinforce the bond with his mother. On the other hand, if he married a woman who had no ties with his mother, and if after marriage the couple settled somewhere far away, the mother and son would retain their relationship on the ground of pure love and duty, while the emotional ties based on attachment would be weakened.

In the ensuing months I watched as the saint skillfully created a situation in which the young man lost his interest in the woman with strong ties to his mother's relatives. Soon afterwards he married someone else and settled in a city far away from where his mother lived. Immediately his health improved.

In this case it was in the young man's destiny to be united with someone in marriage. All the saint did was create a situation in which he married a young woman who was destined to have a long-lasting marital relationship with a healthy man. By tying the tentacles of the young man's secondary karmas to hers, the saint helped to modify his health-related destiny without disturbing the mother's main prarabdha karma, which was to be separated from her son.

But how could ordinary people know that the bride had a healthy husband as part of her destiny, or that one of the strong influences on the young man's state of health was the mother's destiny to be separated from her son? The truth is, we can never be certain, because it is impossible for us to know which particular karma is primary and which secondary, nor is it possible to verify that someone's karma has been altered. The saint, however, was endowed with great knowledge and intuitive wisdom, and this was borne out by the fact that the young man's health improved remarkably after his marriage.

But my personal faith in that saint and my own conclusions are not sufficient to explain the dynamics of karma in regard to such complex issues as whether or not our karma can be shared by others, or whether in addition to personal karmas we also share group karmas. If that is so, what are the logistics behind it? Further, the justice in reaping what we sow is obvious, but where is the justice in reaping the fruits of group karmas which we may not have personally sown? The scriptures entertain such questions and explain these relationships.

They tell us that, with the exception of meditative karmas, there is no such thing as totally personal karmas. All actions involve at least two parties: the one who performs the action, and the person or object affected by the action. And because both parties to an action are connected to other parties, the ripple effect causes several parties to become involved in actions and their fruition. As long as we have a body and live in the world, it is utterly impossible to live in karmic isolation. Even entering the world involves at least three parties: the mother, the father, and the one being born. All have their independent destiny as well as a shared group destiny. One person's main destiny functions as another's secondary karmas, and vice versa. Thus we are all caught in a complex karmic web. Hundreds of stories documented in the epic literature explain the complex nature of destiny in an understandable fashion. Let's look at one from the *Ramayana*.

Rama was a prince born in the city of Ayodhya to King Dhasharatha and Queen Kausalya, and when he grew into manhood he married Princess Sita. On the day he was to have been crowned king, he was instead sent into exile for fourteen years. His wife and his brother Lakshmana followed him to share his exile. Soon after, unable to bear the pain of separation from his son, the king died. Rama's misfortunes deepened when Sita was abducted by Ravana, the king of Sri Lanka. But with the help of the Vanaras (a tribe whose faces resembled monkeys), Rama vanquished Ravana and freed his wife. Finally, after completing the term of exile, the couple returned to Ayodhya, where Rama assumed the throne.

Throughout his exile Rama experienced tremendous ups and downs, comforts and discomforts, losses and gains. He helped many people, and he killed many people. To understand his destiny and its relationship with the destiny of those whose lives intertwined with his, we have to know what happened in his previous life, when he existed in the form of Narayana.

Kama (desire) is accompanied by an army of lust and other charms and temptations, and it has besieged many masters, among them Buddha and Christ. It once waged battle against the illustrious sage Narada when he was in deep samadhi. But Narada, the most beloved disciple of Narayana, was able to remain unperturbed. Kama recognized his defeat and retreated.

Narada was happy with his accomplishment, but when he told Shiva about his victory, Shiva smiled and advised him not to talk about this in front of his master, because Narayana did not like even the subtlest traces of ego. Narada made no reply to Shiva, but he did not think his victory over Kama had fed his ego.

Narada then went to Narayana, and in the course of conversation he said, "Through your grace I remained unperturbed when Kama attacked me during my samadhi."

With a smile Narayana responded, "How can Kama have any effect on an accomplished sage like you? I am very glad, Narada." And with these words, he dismissed his disciple.

Narada was an unsurpassed master of astrology and palmistry. One day the king sent for him and asked him to help in shaping the future of his adult daughter. Her horoscope indicated that she was the most beautiful, intelligent, loving, and venerable woman in the world. She would marry a man of supreme beauty and strength. Her husband would be omniscient and immortal. All the great qualities and virtues, known and unknown to humankind, would reside in the couple. Narada had never seen such an exceptional horoscope. He decided to double-check his interpretation by reading the princess' palm, so the king sent for his daughter.

The princess was the embodiment of supreme beauty, and when she walked into the room Narada was overwhelmed. When he took her hand to look at her palm his entire consciousness dissolved at her touch. He saw that her palm matched her horoscope. Although he kept his composure outwardly, inwardly Narada was melting. He was hopelessly in love, but he calmly advised the royal family to invite the most eligible men from the kingdom, and from neighboring kingdoms as well, to attend her *svayamvara*—a ceremony in which a princess chooses her own husband.

At the same time, he began to devise a strategy for marrying her himself. He did not have the qualities of the husband described in the horoscope, but he was confident that he could gain them through the grace of his master. So he went straight to Narayana and explained the situation. Narayana blessed him with a beautiful body, virility, strength, and youth. However, unbeknownst to Narada, Narayana also gave him the face of a monkey.

With a high heart and great hopes, Narada returned to the palace on the day of the ceremony and took his place with the other candidates. He noticed that two of them were watching him and exchanging sardonic glances, and when the princess arrived she, too, gave him an odd look—and passed him by. He was enraged and stormed out.

With shattered hopes and a wrathful heart he stalked through the countryside. After a while he saw that the two candidates he had noticed earlier were following him. Struggling to regain his equilibrium, he asked them who they were and why they had mocked him at the ceremony. They said they had been sent by Shiva to keep an eye on him and, laughing, told him to look at his reflection in the nearby lake. The moment Narada saw his monkey face, he exploded. Turning on Shiva's students, he shouted, "May you live like demons despite all your knowledge and yogic powers!"

Now Narada's anger turned toward his master, and he started for the ashram. On the way, he met Narayana walking with the princess. That increased his fury, and with no preamble he shouted, "You are dishonest and deceitful! You hypocrite! You cannot stand the thought of anyone being happy. I will teach you a lesson. Hear my curse: Just as today I am suffering on account of losing my wife, you will one day suffer the loss of your wife. And only those who have monkey faces will be able to help you."

Instead of answering wrath with wrath, Narayana replied with great love, "I accept this curse. To save you from long-lasting misery, I acted as I did."

Then Narada realized that he had made a mistake. Falling at Narayana's feet, he begged forgiveness and asked permission to withdraw the curse. But Narayana said, "No. For the sake of preserving your willpower intact, I will take this curse upon myself. It will be honored when I incarnate as Rama. At that time I will also redeem Shiva's students from your curse."

About this time, two great yogis, Manu and his wife, Shatarupa, were ruling a great kingdom. They wanted to have Narayana as their own son in another lifetime, so they handed their kingdom over to their eldest son and dedicated their lives to meditating on Narayana. After several years, Narayana appeared and granted the boon they were seeking. Thus Manu and Shatarupa reincarnated as King Dhasharatha and his queen, Kausalya, Rama's parents.

As a young man, Prince Dhasharatha was an expert archer, famous for his ability to hit a moving target without seeing it—all he needed was to hear it. One night he went hunting in the forest. A young saint, accompanying his blind parents on a holy pilgrimage, was camping on the outskirts of that forest. Leaving his parents in camp, he went to look for water. As he knelt beside a nearby pond to fill his vessel, the flowing water sounded like an animal drinking—and Prince Dhasharatha, who was nearby, released an arrow at the source of the sound. But when the arrow found its mark, the prince was startled to hear a human cry.

Prince Dhasharatha rushed to the spot, and found the young saint dying. With his last breath, the young saint asked the prince to find his parents and care for them. The distraught prince agreed to this. He found the blind couple, told them what had happened, and begged for their forgiveness. But instead of granting it, the father cursed Dhasharatha, saying, "My grief is so great that it will soon kill me. May grief over your son end your life as well."

Eventually, Dhasharatha inherited his father's kingdom, married, and had four sons. Rama was the eldest and the most beloved. When the king announced that he was turning the kingdom over to Rama, everyone was overjoyed—except the king's second wife. Instead of rejoicing, she demanded that the day intended for Rama's coronation be the day of his exile, and that her son, who was out of the kingdom, be crowned as soon as he returned. Because of a vow he had sworn to her years before, the king had to grant her wish, but the pain of losing his son Rama was so overwhelming that King Dhasharatha died of grief.

Rama spent the next twelve years roaming in the forest in exile with his wife, Sita, and his brother, Lakshmana, facing hunger, thirst, wild beasts, and cannibal tribes. During the thirteenth year, when they were living in the forests of south India on the banks of the Godawari River, Supanakha, the princess of Sri Lanka, visited Rama's ashram and instantly fell in love with him. Rama told her he had taken a vow that Sita would be his only wife, and therefore it was impossible for him to marry her. But Supanakha would not accept this and made several vain attempts to seduce him. Finally she resorted to threats, telling Rama that her brother, Ravana, the mighty king of Sri Lanka, would force him to marry her. She then attacked Sita. Lakshmana instantly sprang forward and cut off Supanakha's nose. Seething with frustration and bent on revenge, the disfigured princess fled to her brother's kingdom.

Hiding her infatuation with Rama, Supanakha lied to her brother, saying that Rama had cut off her nose as a challenge to him. She convinced Ravana that Rama was as proud of his beautiful wife as he was of his own strength, and that it would be a disgrace to Sri Lanka and its king if Rama were not brought low by separating him from his wife and defeating him on the battlefield. So with the help of his crafty allies, Ravana abducted Sita and carried her to his capital. And when Sita persistently refused to marry him, he imprisoned her in his palace garden.

Distraught, Rama and Lakshmana searched the forest, but found no trace of Sita. Eventually they learned that Ravana had abducted her, but they did not know where to find Ravana until their search led them to the kingdom of the Vanaras, a group of people whose faces resembled the faces of monkeys. The king and his chiefs became Rama's friends and allies, and with their help Rama located Sita. After a long and costly war, Rama defeated Ravana and was reunited with his wife.

This story gives us a glimpse of the web of destiny. Rama's was woven from many threads, the main ones being the boon he had granted his parents in their previous lifetime by agreeing to be their son, the effects of Narada's curse, and his own promise to redeem the two students of Shiva who were also under Narada's curse. There were hundreds of others involved in Rama's life either as friends or enemies, and according to the scriptures, all of their destinies were connected to Rama's destiny. Rama, a highly evolved soul, had no personal karma and therefore no karmic reason to be born or to die. But he used the boons which he granted and the curses that he accepted to create a momentary web of destiny in order to help disentangle others from their karmic webs. While he was caught in his own karmic web, however, he suffered anguish and enjoyed pleasure, just as ordinary mortals do.

While Rama rode the karmic roller coaster, he never lost his inner awareness. One rainy day during the time Sita was being held captive, Narada visited the heartbroken Rama. Knowing that Rama was suffering because of the curse he had uttered, Narada said, "I have been your devoted student and servant. You knew my weakness, and still you let my weakness stretch as far as this. Why?"

Rama replied, "One of us had to go through this karmic

turmoil. In my case, it will be finished in a couple of years, whereas you would have been entangled for several lifetimes. Furthermore, I honored the law of karma by rewarding my parents, who in their previous lifetime had performed intense austerities and meditation in order to have me as their son. And once I became their son, the karmic strand of my destiny became associated with the destiny of my parents, and with all those who were connected to them. Look at the rewarding part of my destiny. The exile gave me an opportunity to be in the company of many enlightened sages, who, like my parents, had been meditating on me."

As this story illustrates, masters like Narayana are able to take on the karmas of others. Further, they have the ability either to attenuate or to maximize the strength of the karmas they take on. Because of the knowledge they possess, they maintain their equilibrium while the karmic storm runs its course.

Rama's destiny consisted of extraordinary karmas which he consciously created out of previous karmic influences. Our karmas are of a different sort. Our current actions are motivated by the central and secondary strands of our destiny. At the time of performing actions—and right before—our minds are affected by like and dislike, love and hatred, attraction and repulsion. Karmas caused by such actions are not the same as the ones Rama used to weave his destiny. We ordinary people have no free will in deciding which karmic strands to use as the main strand of destiny and which are to be secondary.

But as an enlightened being Rama had the freedom to decide when, where, and how the karmas he took on would manifest. His story illustrates the interconnectedness of karmas between individuals and groups, but it does not entirely clarify the process by which the karmas of ordinary people are ordered. So let us now turn our attention to another story, which will shed light on how one particular karma becomes the leading force in an individual's destiny and eventually overpowers all other karmas.

Once there lived a murderous robber, notorious as much for his cruelty as for his cleverness. No one's life or property was safe when he was around. One night his gang attacked an isolated village, but instead of finding easy pickings, they found themselves outnumbered, and after a long fight they scattered into the forest. Separated from his fellows, the leader was soon completely lost.

While he was trying to get his bearings, he heard the wail of someone in pain, and going toward the sound he came upon a lone woman in the process of giving birth. Summer was at its height, and the woman was desperately thirsty. For some unknown reason, the robber felt compassion for her. He gave her water and helped her deliver her child.

While assisting her, he found himself remembering that he too had been born and that his mother had gone through similar birth pains. This line of thought led him to reflect on the preciousness of human life and how he had done nothing in his life but bring pain and suffering to others. This realization totally transformed him. Right there and then, he decided to change his life. Disregarding the danger to himself, he carried the woman and her child back to the village and was killed by the angry and vengeful villagers.

After death the robber was brought to Samyamani Puri, the realm where conscience alone rules, to face Yama, the king of death. Yama's secretary opened the book of karmas and informed him that based on the law of karma, the ex-cutthroat was entitled to seven thousand years of hell. However, saving the woman and child, and sacrificing his own life in the process, entitled him to be the king of heaven for one day. The question was, which should come first—hell or heaven?

Suddenly Deva Guru, the celestial teacher, appeared and said that even though quantitatively the cutthroat's good karma was minute, it was intensely potent. And according to the law of karma established at the beginning of creation, such intensely potent karmas become the most powerful forces in the formation of destiny. Therefore, this man had earned the right to be king of heaven before he had to reap the fruit of his other karmas.

Then, the instant the former robber became king of heaven his consciousness expanded greatly, and bowing his head to the celestial teacher, he sought his guidance. The teacher explained that there are two ways of living in heaven: enjoy its pleasures, or use them selflessly. "Once the karmas that brought you here are exhausted," the teacher said, "you will have to attend to your remaining karmas, but for one day all celestial wealth and property belongs to you. It is your choice to either enjoy them for your personal pleasure or use them to serve others."

The king of heaven understood, and immediately started giving heavenly objects away. He gave the celestial trees to sage Kashyapa; the gems he gave to Bhrigu; the horses went to Atri; and the elephants to Marichi. He worked so hard that by the end of the day he had nothing left for himself.

Yama's secretary looked into the karmic record again, and found that this man was now entitled to thousands of years of heaven. He gladly accepted, surrendering his entire power and privilege to the celestial teacher, and asked him for further guidance. And when he learned from his teacher that the fruit of renunciation knows no boundaries, he renounced heaven itself and set his foot on the path of spiritual practice.

According to scriptures such as the *Yoga Sutra* it is possible to create a powerful positive karma which overrides other karmas. The karmas generated through such means become the main strands of our destiny. Similarly, we create a powerful negative karma by hurting someone who is filled with fear or is sick, someone who is a miser, someone who trusts us, or one who is totally dedicated to spiritual life. This negative karma, too, overrides all other karmas. The scriptures are replete with examples of those who were entangled in the web of destiny just as we are, but who created powerful karmas which overrode many aspects of that destiny for better or worse. In other words, the intense karmas they created in the present changed the direction of their destiny.

The law of karma is thus both inspiring and discouraging. "Do good, reap good" sounds encouraging. But when we seem to be victims of our past karmas, even though most of us have no idea what they are, the same law is discouraging. Exceptional karmas, however, can be created through intense mantra sadhana, tapas, samadhi, meditation on God, the grace of God, selfless service, the blessings of the adepts, and the company of saints—and these karmas can override destiny. In other words, there are loopholes in the law of karma. Understanding them and learning the techniques for gaining access to them can deliver us from its bondage.

CHAPTER FIVE

LOOPHOLES IN THE LAW OF KARMA

THE PURPOSE OF DESTINY is to determine when we will die and when and how we will be born. The goal of yoga is to attain the highest state of samadhi (spiritual absorption), known as *nirbija* (seedless) samadhi, for in this state we are totally free from the subtle traces of our karmas (*Yoga Sutra* 1:18,51). Then if all karmic seeds are destroyed, we attain freedom from the cycle of death and birth and all that lies in between. We also gain perfect vision, the highest form of intuitive knowledge, and come to know the truth in its fullness; we become adept—a yogi in the fullest sense of the word. We have reached a realm which shines through its own intrinsic light.

The scriptures recount stories of adepts who have attained complete freedom from their karmic traces and have consequently risen above the law of karma and the world ruled by it. They have reached such a high state of freedom that, while living in the realm of divine providence, they can create or dismantle karmic strands at will. Their destiny is dead and they have become immortal. With the disappearance of karma and destiny, their intuitive wisdom is no longer obstructed and they can see the karmas and destinies of others clearly. This gives them the ability to detect the loopholes in the law of karma and to use these loopholes to serve others. From time to time they descend from the realm of divine providence to help and guide those caught in the karmic whirlpool. To see how this is done, let's turn to the following story.

———

In the fifteenth century in the city of Banaras there lived two great saints, Tulsidas and Baba Kinaram, both famous for their miraculous powers and believed to be enlightened masters.

One day a barren woman went to see Tulsidas, hoping he would bless her so that she could conceive, for in the cultural system of that time it was a disgrace for a woman to be without a child—such a disgrace, in fact, that it was considered a sin to even look on the face of a barren woman. Through his intuitive power Tulsidas saw that the woman's destiny did not reveal a single karmic strand which would make her a mother, either in this lifetime or in the next seven. So he sent her away, saying he could not help her because there was no child in her destiny.

Not willing to give up, the woman next visited Baba Kinaram and told him what Tulsidas had said. Baba Kinaram confirmed Tulsidas' finding. With all hope gone, the woman burst into tears, sobbing that since she had no place in society, it was better that she die. Baba Kinaram took pity on her, and after meditating for a few minutes, he said lovingly, "Do not worry, Mother. Come with me."

He led her to a neem tree in his ashram, one he had

planted and tended for years. "You have hundreds of children," he said to the tree. "Please share one of them with this woman. Her descendants will take care of your children."

Then, after a few minutes of silence, he told the woman that she would soon have a child. In due course she gave birth to a healthy boy and brought him to Baba Kinaram to express her gratitude.

Tulsidas, who lived nearby, heard about this and was puzzled. Her destiny had clearly shown that this woman was not destined to have a child. So he went into deep meditation to find out how the barren woman came to have a baby, but he could not see the reason. Finally he turned his consciousness toward God, who explained: "After investigating and not finding a baby in her destiny, Baba Kinaram asked me to bless her with a child. And when I told him I could not give her what she was not destined to have, Baba Kinaram argued with me, saying that I was a useless God if all I could provide was what destiny already had in store. Why would people waste their time loving, serving, and meditating on me in that case? So I guided him to the neem tree, which through my inspiration gladly agreed to give this woman one of her children."

Baba Kinaram's life was full of such miracles. When he first visited Banaras as a wandering sadhu, no one but another great master, Baba Kaluram, recognized him. To confirm that Baba Kinaram was the great saint he had been waiting for, Baba Kaluram asked him to bring him a fish for his meal. Baba Kinaram simply stepped into the Ganges and asked the river to give him a fish. Instantly, one sprang into his hand. He cooked it and served it to Baba Kaluram as instructed. But when he saw the fish, Baba Kaluram said, "I am no longer hungry; give the fish back to the Ganges." When Baba

Kinaram picked up the plate, the fish came to life, and he put it back in the Ganges.

On another occasion, when Baba Kinaram was roaming in a Muslim kingdom where sadhus were banned, he was arrested. The prisoners had to work grinding grain, but when Baba Kinaram was given this task, he simply said *Chal re chakari,* "Grinding stones, start moving!" The stones began to rotate and didn't stop. When the king heard about this, he came to the prison, apologized to Baba Kinaram, and set him free, granting his request to release all the other prisoners as well.

Reweaving Destiny

Now the question is: Why do the prayers of an adept like Baba Kinaram work, while ours do not? The answer is clear: such masters are free from "here" and fully connected "there." With the sword of knowledge, they have cut the rope of karma and burned it in their yogic fire. Primordial nature, prakriti, has withdrawn its veil from their third eye, the seat of intuitive knowledge. They are not motivated by reward or punishment, and yet they are always in the service of the Divine Being. Nature finds great pleasure in serving such adepts.

Just as we can see physical objects through our eyes, these masters are able to see the subtle forces of the senses, mind, ego, and intellect, as well as the unconscious mind and the subtle impressions stored there. The fourth dimension— time—is as clearly visible to them as the objects of the three-dimensional world are to us. By paying attention to the time principle they can clearly see what we have done in our past, because our actions, as well as their results, are subject to the forces of time and space. That is why yogis say that every object and the experience related to it is conditioned by time, space, and the causal force behind the object and the experience. These three—time, space, and causation—are inextricably linked. The yogis who have transcended the realm of time and space can clearly see the causal seeds—the destiny—of other beings whose consciousness still operates within the realm of time, space, and causation. These yogis alone can detect the loopholes in the law of karma.

A detective does not investigate a case without a reason; similarly, an adept does not try to find a loophole in the law of karma without a reason. When called upon by divine providence, the adepts pay attention to the karmic strands of someone's destiny, and if possible they simply reorder these strands to bring about the effect desired. For example, in the story in chapter two of the brahmin and his horse, the sage Narada guided the brahmin to sell the horse, thereby creating a vacuum that had to be filled by another horse, and this created prosperity where there had been none before. In that case it was not necessary for Narada to find a loophole—all he did was discover a system of managing destiny wisely. In the case of the barren woman, however, Baba Kinaram went a little further. He had to find another way to manage karmic strands, because the woman had no child in her destiny at all. But with Baba Kinaram's intervention, the neem tree shared one of her children, and in return the descendants of that woman became the caretakers of neem trees. This reciprocal relationship upheld the law of karma by intertwining the destinies of the tree and the woman's descendants, thereby creating a situation for each to give and receive.

Similarly, as we saw in the previous chapter, Narayana used Narada's curse and the austerities of Manu and Shatarupa as the karmic strands of his destiny to incarnate as Rama. But sometimes it is necessary to create entirely new karmic strands, as was the case when the sage Durvasa had to discover a sophisticated way to reweave the fabric of destiny when five souls who, like Narayana, were free from all karmas decided to incarnate as children of Kunti.

———

Kunti was destined to be blessed with these five children, but her husband's destiny was to die if he had a sexual relationship with his wife. Kunti's destiny also dictated that she would be such a loyal wife that she would not even think of another man. So in order to bring these five souls to this world in as human a manner as possible, sage Durvasa visited Kunti's father when she was still a teenager. Kunti served as a gracious hostess to Durvasa during his stay with her father. When the visit was ending and Durvasa was taking his leave of the family, he told Kunti that he was greatly pleased with the service she had rendered him during his stay, and invited her to ask anything of him, promising her that whatever she wished for would be granted. In her innocence, Kunti told the sage that she did not know what to ask for; finally she said simply, "Please give me anything you think I will need in my life." Durvasa gave her a mantra and explained the method of practicing it, as well as its intended effect. He said that through its power she could invoke any of the forces of nature, and that whatever force she invoked would be bound to fulfill her desire at once.

Several years later Kunti was married to the virtuous and noble emperor of north India, King Pandu. She soon realized that she would lose her husband if he slept with her, and that he was worried about not having an heir to his throne. So one

day she told him about the mantra she had received from sage
Durvasa and the power it contained. King Pandu was overjoyed. He immediately asked her to use the mantra to invoke
Dharma, the cosmic counterpart of truth and virtue which
resides in all individual beings, and to ask for a son. So Kunti
meditated on the mantra, intent on Dharma, and the divine
force appeared. Dharma knew why she had invoked its presence, and instantly granted her a son. Later, on different occasions, she received the blessings of four other divine forces.
Altogether she was blessed with five mighty and noble sons,
who later became friends of Lord Krishna and were instru-
mental in establishing justice and righteousness. Even today,
hundreds of shrines and holy places are associated with their
memories.

———

The sage Durvasa created a new karmic strand because he
had the capacity to see the destinies of King Pandu and Queen
Kunti, and because he was also able to place their destinies in
the context of the welfare of humanity. He knew that no man
other than King Pandu was destined to marry Kunti, who was
so evolved in her own right that her association with anyone
not equal to him in virtue and wisdom would be an insult to
her destiny. Divine providence had chosen Kunti to be the
mother of five highly evolved souls, so the service rendered
by Kunti to sage Durvasa created a new space in her destiny,
which Durvasa filled with the power of mantra. In other
words, by letting her serve him, sage Durvasa created an
opportunity to add something to her destiny which was not
there before. This particular karma was free-floating and
powerful, and Kunti now had the freedom to choose when
and where to connect it to the main strand of her destiny.

There are situations, however, in which there is no room for creating new karmic strands to connect to the main strand of destiny. In such cases, sages like Durvasa may intervene directly—but only under divine guidance. For example, if someone's destined life span has run its course, but their continued presence can ease the pains of millions, then these sages may decide to intervene in the law of karma. The story of Shankaracharya's life, well known in the spiritual tradition of India, illustrates how a sage can intervene in the law of karma for the greater good of humanity.

———

The great master Shankaracharya was born in south India in the eighth century A.D. At a very early age he mastered the Sanskrit language and the scriptures—a task that normally takes many years of intense study. When he was still a child he left his home in the pursuit of enlightenment, met his master, and received initiation. By the time he was twelve he had become one of the most prominent spiritual leaders of his day.

This great adept had a profound understanding of the dynamics of destiny and knew that he had a total of only sixteen years to live. He worked without ceasing to complete his life's mission within the allotted time; and when his time to die had come, he made plans to cast off his body in the high peaks of the Himalayas. He was seated in a cave near Badrinath, preparing to return the elements of his body back to their source, when Sage Vyasa arrived and argued that his mission was not complete, that he had only laid the groundwork. "What good is a mission which dies out as soon as you leave your body?" he asked. "You must stay and train those who can continue your work after you are gone."

To this, Shankaracharya replied, "I agree with what you

say. But how can I remain in a body which I am supposed to use for only sixteen years?"

"I will give you sixteen years of my own life," Vyasa replied. And so Shankaracharya lived sixteen more years, teaching the gospel of unitary consciousness, training students, and writing commentaries on the scriptures, as well as independent texts. He left his body at the age of thirty-two.

How can anybody give part of their life to someone else? What does it mean? Since birth in a particular species and the life span in that particular body are totally dependent on destiny, how can longevity, which is interwoven with the stream of time, be split and shared with someone else? In this case, by giving him sixteen years of his own life, Vyasa shared his destiny with Shankaracharya. He did not rearrange the strands of secondary karmas, help him exchange or link his karmas to those of another person, or create a new karma to attach to the main strand of his destiny. Instead, Vyasa extended Shankaracharya's destiny by adding his own to it. All along, Shankaracharya had possessed the capacity to extend his own life, but he did not do so. His karmic obligations were complete and he was personally free from the law of karma, but he still accepted his destiny. Only when divine providence motivated Vyasa to intervene did Shankaracharya agree to stay in the body.

Sometimes, instead of detecting loopholes in the law of karma, or creating new karmic strands, or intervening directly in someone's karma, a great master will create a situation in which someone can get in touch with their own spiritual samskaras and spontaneously strengthen them. The next story explains how the unconscious contents of the mind come forward at the time of death, how the most powerful samskara takes the lead, and how an enlightened master can help us at that time.

———

There once lived a young man named Ajamil, whose father was one of the teachers for the royal family, and thus a wealthy man. Hoping that his son would someday inherit his position, he sent Ajamil to a famous learning center *(gurukula),* where the teachers soon realized he was a genius. His mind was so penetrating that even as a student he was a step ahead of his teachers. And due to his indomitable will, no one could stop him once he had decided to do something.

During the final years of his education, the wisest among all the teachers took Ajamil under his personal supervision. With his yogic powers he made an inventory of Ajamil's interior life, and through intuitive diagnosis clearly saw that Ajamil had been a great yogi and devotee of Bhagavan Narayana, the primordial divine master, for several lifetimes. And because of his previous yoga practice, Ajamil had a perfectly one-pointed and steady mind. Deep in his heart dwelt the Lord of Life, Narayana. Along with this samskara, however, the wise teacher noticed a powerful samskara of lust and realized that Ajamil was fully equipped to fall into its grip: he had ample wealth, the company of youthful members of the royal household, a charming personality, the vigor of youth, a strong will, and a one-pointed mind.

It was customary in those days for students to go out asking for alms, but the teacher made sure that Ajamil visited only places that were free from distractions. Further, he told Ajamil clearly that he must not go into town during his time as a student. If for some reason he should need to visit his father or the palace, he must not pass through certain streets.

Ajamil did not take his teacher's advice seriously. One day as he passed along one of the streets that his teacher had told him to avoid, he heard an enticing melody issuing from a house, so he decided to stop and ask for alms. A beautiful woman opened the door and let him in. She was a skilled courtesan, and he was captivated the moment he crossed her threshold. When Ajamil returned to his school later than usual that day, his teacher knew instantly what had happened. He forbade Ajamil to leave the campus and tried everything he knew to help the young man drop this experience from his mind. But it soon became apparent that these efforts were in vain.

When Ajamil finished his studies he rejoined his family. Now he had both the freedom to spend time with the courtesan and the money to lavish on her. Even though his parents arranged his marriage to a beautiful and loyal woman, he showed no interest in a marital relationship. Soon after Ajamil's wedding his father died, and he inherited the position of teacher to the king's children. Because his association with the royal family brought him into public view, his relationship with the courtesan quickly became common knowledge. The king was embarrassed, but because Ajamil's father had been his friend, he too tried to dissuade the young man from his dissolute way of life. When his entreaties failed, the king was forced to expel him from the court.

Ajamil had inherited his father's wealth, so he did not particularly care that he had lost his job. He continued to lavish his riches on wine, women, and song. He isolated himself from good society, and society in turn abandoned him. In time, the courtesan grew to love him and bore him several children, but by then both his money and his youth were spent. Finally, unable to bear the pain of poverty and humiliation, Ajamil left with the courtesan and her children. But wherever he went in search of a livelihood, the story of his fallen character had preceded him. He was ostracized everywhere and was forced to live as an outcast.

So Ajamil built a hut in the forest and adopted the life of a hunter. Tormented by hunger, fatigue, worry, and guilt, he aged quickly and his health began to fail. His younger children depended on him for food and shelter; the older ones blamed him for their pains and miseries. Still, the power of lust was so strong that the former courtesan kept having children.

Several decades had passed since Ajamil had been in school and in the presence of a wise man, but one day the sage Narada, who was passing through the forest, stopped at Ajamil's hut for alms at a time when Ajamil was brooding about his life, his karmas, and their consequences. Narada's voice soothed his senses but saddened his heart. He was overwhelmed that a civilized person—a sage, at that—had stopped at his hut, but he was embarrassed because he had nothing to offer him except a little pigeon flesh. The woman, however, had been saving a fistful of millet for just such an emergency, so she cooked it and offered it to Narada. Satisfied, the sage decided to rest in the hut for a while with Ajamil.

When he heard Ajamil's story, Narada offered his wise counsel. "Remember, you are a learned man," he said. "Disidentify yourself from this present misery and follow the path of meditation and austerity. Your soul is ever pure; it is totally unaffected by your actions and their fruits. Forget this world. Remember the name of Narayana, and recapture the light which has become veiled within you."

But Ajamil argued, "When do I have time to remember anybody, including God? Either I am sick or I am out hunting for food for my children. How can I abandon them? I must be faithful to my duty. And this woman, although once a prostitute, has sacrificed her comfortable life for me, and I must care for her. The older children are big enough to fend for themselves, but the little ones will die if I leave this household in search of God."

While Narada was contemplating how to help Ajamil, he noticed that the woman was pregnant, and a perfect plan flashed in his mind. Turning to the woman, he said, "My daughter, you seem to be glowing. It must be due to the wonderful soul that has entered your womb. Come closer and let me look at your palms."

Narada matched her palm with Ajamil's and exclaimed joyfully, "How blessed you both are. The baby has brought with him the light of God. Now I advise you, Ajamil, not to hunt any more after the baby is born. Instead, you should stay home and take care of your son. I will again come to you for the naming ceremony of this child." After this, Narada walked into the forest singing the glory of God.

When the baby was born, true to his word, Narada returned and named the infant Narayana. He played with it as though he were playing with God in baby form. Ajamil lost his worries and concerns, intoxicated as he was with the divine aroma that emanated from Narada. The sage intensified Ajamil's experience by repeating the name "Narayana" again and again while he played with the infant. Thus, subtly and skillfully Narada initiated Ajamil without Ajamil's realizing what was happening.

Now frail and old, Ajamil played with the newborn baby

while the rest of the family gathered food and firewood. All day long he sat next to the infant, repeating his name: "Narayana, Narayana." Eventually the word, although apparently directed to the baby, began to connect itself with the memory of the divinity corresponding to it that was stored in Ajamil's unconscious mind.

Within a year Ajamil became mortally ill; shortly before death came, he started experiencing the struggle among different thoughts and memories. His conscience presented him with the subtle impressions of his lifelong deeds, and he was terrified. Worst among them was guilt. However, along with the streams of painful memories there also flowed the memory of the infant Narayana. Gradually the subtle impressions created by the word "Narayana" and the divinity identical to it became so powerful that the baby's association with the word vanished. The radiant, divine light emanating from "Narayana" burned all of Ajamil's karmas and their corresponding subtle impressions, and he left his body with full awareness of his destination. Using the word "Narayana" as a boat, he navigated the river of the unconscious mind, and leaving the islands of both heaven and hell behind, he reached the shore of everlasting light. The scriptures call this place *vaikuntha dhama*.

The scriptures are replete with examples of sages—Narada, Durvasa, Dattatreya, Hanuman, Gorakha Natha, and dozens of others—who came to the rescue of those whose lives had been touched by the grace of God but who had become momentarily caught in a karmic whirlpool. By intervening, these sages served as conduits of divine grace.

Narada intervened in this instance because he noticed that

Ajamil had a powerful spiritual samskara which had been veiled by the samskara of lust and self-indulgence. So Narada created a situation in which Ajamil could get in touch with his spiritual samskaras and, by spontaneously strengthening them, conquer other samskaras and karmas which otherwise would have dominated his mind-field during the time of his death.

If we delve deeper into the law of karma and its relationship with divine help, we see that neither Narada's visit to Ajamil nor Ajamil's strong attachment to the child Narayana was accidental. The dominance of "Narayana-consciousness" during the time of his final departure was not accidental either. Ajamil was an extraordinarily brilliant man, and once the force of his genius, one-pointed mind, and indomitable will began to flow in the direction of sensual pleasure, no one could stop him, including his wise teacher and the king. But once he had learned his lesson and become disgusted with both the world and himself, he reached a turning point. Had Ajamil not already been blessed with the grace of Narayana, Narada would not have entered his life. And without Narada, Ajamil would have fallen into deep depression and dejection—he would have drowned in never-ending grief.

The saints tells us that a human being cannot have right thinking or make right resolution without *satsanga* (the company of wise people), and that it is impossible to be blessed with satsanga without the grace of God. Even though God's grace is unconditional, they say, a person becomes worthy of containing it through good karmas. These in turn instigate the events that lead to the sages intervening with destiny on the behalf of divine providence. We meet such blessed ones at the turning points in our lives, and under their guidance we strengthen our illuminating samskaras. As we do this, our worldly samskaras fade away, so that at the time of our departure it is the illuminating samskaras that propel the wheel of life.

In the example we have just seen, when Ajamil turned his face toward Narayana, he never looked back at the world. The forces of sharpened intellect, one-pointed mind, and indomitable will he once employed for self-indulgence were all directed toward Narayana-consciousness. Not the slightest thought or feeling unrelated to Narayana lingered at the time of his death. Thus after death Ajamil entered *vaikuntha dhama,* the realm of reality where the cycle of death and birth totally ceases. This realm shines with its own inherent effulgence. This realm is also known as *goloka dhama,* the realm accessible only to those who have transcended sense cravings, the realm in which the soul delights in its self-nature.

Finding Our Own Way Out

The sages' way of working with the karmas of others helps us gain an understanding of what karma is and how it shapes our destiny; their stories strengthen our conviction that there are great masters who can help us if we are fully connected to them, and if there is a divine reason compelling them to do so. But this does not really help us attain freedom from the bondage of karma. Divine intervention is very rare. Even though all religions acknowledge the existence of guardian angels and saints who are said to be blessed with the power to relieve human suffering in extraordinary ways, humanity at large is still embroiled in intense pain and misery. That is why yogis adamantly advise us: "Enlighten yourself, for no one else can give you salvation."

Transcending the law of karma is the ultimate goal of yoga; yoga practices and techniques are the means of reaching this goal. These practices all have one purpose in common: to transform our habits and wash off negative impressions stored in the unconscious mind because, according to yogis, karmic impressions formed in the past occupy our mind-field at the time of death, and this determines what happens next. The world created by these samskaras becomes more real to a dying person than the empirical world they have been experiencing throughout life. And this world is delightful, miserable, or a mixture of both, depending on the nature of these karmic impressions. Those who are dying have usually slipped into this world unconsciously; they do not know how they entered it or how to leave it, and their death and rebirth are therefore unconscious. They are at the mercy of their samskaras because the conscious will is not functioning. That is what yogis call bondage.

For example, attachment to the objects of the world creates a deep sense of fear and insecurity at the time of death because throughout life we have continuously filled our mind with the idea that the objects of the world and the people we love are integral to our existence. When the time comes when we must continue our journey without our family, friends, and possessions, we find ourselves at a loss. Even though we know that the parting is inevitable, we attempt to hold on. We fail—and we are overwhelmed. At that moment—the moment of death—insecurity, frustration, fear, and grief cloud the entire mind-field and become the train of thought on which we are swept into the next realm. The consequences of this are that we helplessly carry these feelings with us and continue suffering on account of them.

To understand this better, let's take a careful look at what happens during the time of death. Obviously, we stop breathing. But before we do, certain signs and symptoms of impending death manifest in the breath when death is the result of a lingering illness or old age. The breath gradually becomes shallow, and the pause between inhalation and exhalation lengthens. Then, as lack of oxygen causes the thinking process to deteriorate, conscious, linear thinking gradually vanishes; awareness begins to shift between the conscious and unconscious states. The conscious mind, which works in coordination with the brain, nervous system, and senses, begins to lose its grip, and the unconscious takes over. The dying person is neither fully conscious nor completely unconscious.

In this confused state we are no longer capable of employing the senses and brain to gather data from the external world and process it in a systematic manner, nor can we consciously and systematically retrieve data from the unconscious. Confusion dominates both the conscious and unconscious minds. Mastery over the self disappears and our sense of self-identity becomes muddled. In this disjointed state the unconscious mind takes over, allowing an entirely different world—one composed of our karmic impressions—to emerge.

At the moment of death there is usually so much pulling and pushing going on in different levels of our being—body, breath, nervous system, and brain, as well as our conscious and unconscious minds—that there is no time to think about philosophy. Any philosophy or faith that has not become an integral part of our psyche during our lifetime fades away. Accumulated samskaras, not only from this lifetime but from all previous lifetimes, spontaneously cloud the mind-field. The strongest samskaras or group of samskaras take the lead.

But if at this juncture we can exercise our power of will and determination and maintain conscious control over ourselves, we can fill our inner realm with the train of thought of our choice. Confusion can exist only when clarity is lacking—clarity is knowledge; confusion is maya (the veil of ignorance). When we realize that death is upon us and that body, breath, and conscious mind are about to fall apart, we can use our chosen train of thought as a vehicle in which to migrate voluntarily from the conscious to the unconscious mind, and this will prevent us from falling into confusion. It will allow us to enter the unconscious not as a slave, but as a master.

If the train of thought we use as a vehicle is imbued with divine awareness, it can illuminate the realm of the unconscious, and we will not fall victim to an apparently random stream of unconscious contents. On the other hand, if we cannot maintain conscious control, we will be totally dependent on the nature of our mind's unconscious contents, which could be heavenly, or hellish, or a mixture of both. That is why the scriptures tell us that our train of thought at the time of death determines where we will go after we die.

The body is like a rented apartment, with nature as the landlord. We dwell in this apartment until our lease is over. During our tenancy we must follow the laws set by nature—violating them causes debility and disease, and this results in eviction. On the other hand, compliance with nature's laws—which includes engendering an attitude of nonviolence, truthfulness, compassion, nonattachment, and nonpossessiveness—creates an environment in which we can live joyfully. We must always maintain the awareness that nothing in this world, including the body, is ours. While we inhabit the body we must discover the purpose of life. And when the lease has expired we must graciously hand the keys of breath over to the landlord.

We must approach the next realm in full awareness that this entire world has come from the Divine, exists in the Divine, and ultimately returns to the Divine. It is crucial that we cultivate the understanding that "In this world I own nothing—all the objects of the world are gifts from the Divine, which I must use to accomplish the higher purpose of life. When the time comes I will leave them behind without clinging to them." If we are established in this awareness, it will grant a great sense of freedom at the time of death, and we can leave this body gracefully. The unconscious mind will be fully illuminated with our self-chosen divine train of thought. Then death is neither frightening nor confusing, and we enter the next realm full of joy and purpose.

For this reason, those who are wise gather their power of will and determination (sankalpa shakti) to create spiritually illuminating samskaras, for if they do so they know that at the time of departure they will walk in the light. Such samskaras are created through the constant practice of yoga, and the more intense and long-lasting the practice, the tighter the grip the resulting samskara will have on the mind. This is why fully realized teachers intuitively survey their students' karmic field of samskaras to assess the depth and breadth of their major samskaras and then impart the exact method of contemplation that will strengthen abhyasa (practice) and vairagya (dispassion). Vairagya eradicates all the conscious and unconscious tendencies which spring forth from powerful negative samskaras. It also erases the samskaras which eclipse the soul, and illuminates the path during the dark night of the soul. Abhyasa is the exact method of spiritual practice which can further deepen the spiritually illuminating samskaras already present.

The scriptures and the learned masters say in one voice that the train of thought at the moment of death also determines the exact nature of the next birth. How we go out determines how we come back. Samskaras dictate the train of thought a person will have at the time of death. They also dictate how the pranic forces will disconnect themselves from the different limbs and organs of the body, which particular *nadis* (energy channels) will become active right before death, and from which of the ten gates in the body our consciousness will depart. In the case of Ajamil, for example, it is said that his soul left the body through the fontanelle, the tenth and highest gate. In the yogic tradition this gate is known as *brahma randhra* or *brahma dvara,* the gateway to supreme consciousness.

Others who, because of their karmic entanglements, cannot reach and hold on to such an exalted state of awareness at the time of death are forced by nature to use one of the other nine gates, which lead to realms still in the domain of the cycle of birth and death. Thus our samskaras, by determining our train of thought at the time of death, also determine which gate we are entitled to use, and therefore where we go after death. The anatomy of death in turn determines the dynamics of our birth. In other words, it is the process of death that contains the key to the mystery of birth, and it is our karmas that determine the anatomy of death.

CHAPTER SIX

THE PROPELLER OF DEATH AND BIRTH

MOST OF THE WORLD'S spiritual traditions hold the belief that our unwholesome actions prevent the grace of God from touching our lives. In the *Yoga Sutra* (2:12–13) Patanjali tells us that birth in a particular species is the result of our previous karmas, which also dictate how long we live in that body and what fate awaits us there. Even traditions that do not entertain the idea of rebirth emphasize the importance of actions (karmas) in determining our destination after death. Hindus, Christians, and Buddhists all believe their saviors to be merciful, forgiving, omniscient, and capable of uplifting all souls, yet people from all three traditions still believe in the existence of hell and limbo. This suggests that there are some who never reach heaven despite God's grace and the savior's efforts. In short, it is our own actions that entitle us to heaven or condemn us to hell.

The yoga scriptures pay little attention to the idea of heaven and hell, but many secular texts—for example, the

Puranas—paint a detailed picture of both realms, holding that after death most souls halt temporarily in one place or the other. Once there, they are assigned varying degrees of pleasure and pain. The pleasures of heaven seem preferable to the tormenting pain of hell, but even heaven is not free from suffering. Those who do not know how to manage jealousy and feelings of inferiority and/or superiority, for instance, still suffer even in heaven when they observe that others are entitled to different degrees of pleasure. Traces of desire and jealousy force such souls to create and cling to their personal hell even while in heaven. When their good karmas are exhausted, each soul falls back into the mortal world. Similarly, those in hell remain there until they have exhausted their bad karmas, and then they, too, are reborn.

From the description of heaven and hell in the Puranas and related texts we can draw the following conclusions:

There are realms of awareness to which we go if we are not reborn right after death.

These realms are not permanent abodes. Unliberated souls may reside there temporarily during the transition from death to rebirth.

The ideas of pleasure and pain, which are simply conditions of the mind, continue to exist in these realms.

Although we reach these realms without a body, the experience of pleasure and pain is more intense there than it is in the mortal world, and this indicates that the mind still has the tools to fulfill its urges or suffer from them.

But do heaven and hell or any other realm in an imperceptible sphere really exist? According to religions, the answer is definitely yes; according to yoga, the answer is both yes and no. The afterlife realms exist for those with a strong belief in them, the yogis say, because through our convictions we shape various realities in the realm of our mind. We fail to live wholly in this realm, however, because of the limitations imposed on us by the phenomenal world, but when we die and lose contact with the phenomenal world these limitations are removed and all that remains is the world of our convictions. Those who see their actions in terms of black and white and who are intent on punishment and reward are bound to go to either hell or heaven. Those whose conscience tells them that most of their actions are not so black and white, while the doctrinaire part of their mind insists that they are, wind up in limbo, known as *preta* or *pishacha yoni*. In the words of the Bhagavad Gita (4:24–25), "Worshipers of ghosts go to the realm of ghosts. Worshipers of the gods go to the realm of the gods. The worshipers of supreme truth, the pure Divine Being, attain the realm of the Divine." Thus, if our conviction dictates that heaven or hell is waiting for us after death, that is where we must go. More precisely: if we are Hindu we must go to the Hindu heaven or hell; if we are Christian we must go to the Christian heaven or hell; and so on.

The secular texts describe heaven and hell in detail, as well as the route leading to these realms. Such texts are, however, not strictly yogic in nature, but are rather a mixture of religious practices, customs, superstitions, dogmas, philosophy, and psychology, along with some yogic disciplines. But if the yogic symbolism contained therein is deciphered properly, they offer a clear explanation of the dynamics of death and birth as well as the force that propels this process.

The Journey to Heaven or Hell

According to the secular texts, death is a systematic process in which the period just preceding the moment we actually die is crucial. This is when the messengers of Yamaraja, the king of death, arrive. Those who have surrendered themselves and all their desires, thoughts, feelings, losses, and achievements to the Divine, however, are visited by messengers of the Divine Being. These are a breed apart from the messengers of the king of death.

With the exception of these blessed ones, every dying person must obey the command of Yamaraja's messengers. We must leave the body behind whether we want to or not, and if we try to cling to the body out of fear, attachment, and desire, nature joins forces with death's messengers and evicts us. Then, accompanied by the messengers, we arrive at a broad river inhabited by all manner of creatures—crocodiles, fish, dolphins, sharks, and even cows. This river has many different crossing points, and the messengers drop us at one without consulting us. They remain on the bank and we have to cross the river on our own.

The river is deep, and when we swim across it we have to confront the creatures who dwell there. Anything can happen—the water may be clean or it may be contaminated; we may get caught in the current or be chased by a crocodile; we may begin to drown and then be suddenly pushed back to the surface by a friendly fish; perhaps the next moment a shark rips away a chunk of flesh. We may notice our friends or our enemies swimming or drowning near us. If we are lucky, the messengers drop us at crossings where there are special cows, intelligent animals who are expert swimmers. They offer their tail as a rope and pull us safely across the river.

Whether our crossing has been easy or difficult, we meet the messengers again on the other shore, and they take us to the city of the king of death, where we are met by his bookkeeper. If our karmic records are clear and straightforward, we are assigned to either heaven or hell. Should our records be complex, or should we dispute them, we are brought to the chamber where Yamaraja sits on his throne. Without either mercy or cruelty and unaffected by sentiment, he looks at our karmic records and weighs the pros and cons. Then he decides where we should go, and his decision is final.

We are then led to specific areas of heaven or hell, some better and some worse. The length of our stay is determined by our karmas. Either by tasting heavenly pleasures or by going through hellish pain, the karmas that brought us here are eventually exhausted. Then we are sent back to the earthly realm to begin life all over again.

The yogis interpret this scenario symbolically. According to their experiences, the messengers of the king of death represent the forces of time. These forces are punctual—time cannot be untimely—and once they have arrived, we cannot avoid feeling their presence. We also know the meaning of their coming: it is time to leave the body and move on.

Desire, worry, insecurity, fear, disease, and old age set the stage for the messengers, but long before they actually arrive we harbor the fear of death at both the conscious and unconscious levels. When death actually comes, these feelings intensify. Those of us who do not willingly accept the message that our time in this body is over die miserably.

There is no alternative to this message, but a strong attachment to our bodies, our families, our friends, and our possessions impels us to cling to life, and this creates a deep sense of fear. Throughout life we have filled our mind with the idea that the objects of the world and the people we love are integral to our existence; now, combined with our fear of the unknown, our fear of losing our relationships and possessions intensifies. Death itself is not painful—it is the fear of loss and the fear of the unknown that torment our mind.

The moment death's messengers, the forces of time, arrive our life-force (prana) recognizes them. Disregarding our desires and wishes, it obeys their command and gradually withdraws from the body, brain, and conscious mind. As it does, our limbs, organs, nervous system, and brain begin to lose their ability to function. Filled with fear and confusion, we desperately attempt to hold on, channeling all our reserve energy to cling to life—but we fail. The connection between the life-force, the body, and the conscious mind is severed. This is the moment of death.

When a dying person tries to cling to life, the process of death is accompanied by internal chaos. There is a tug-of-war as the life-force begins to abandon the body while the individual self tries to pull it back. But death will out: in the midst of this commotion, the pranic force ineluctably continues to withdraw from the system of energy channels.

These energy channels, or *nadis,* meet at various sites in the body. Where three or more nadis come together, they form a wheel of energy, or *chakra.* There are ten principal chakras: *muladhara* at the base of the spine, *svadhishthana* in the pelvic region, *manipura* at the navel center, *anahata* at the heart region, *vishuddha* at the throat, *ajna* at the center between the eyebrows, and *vhrikuti, trikuti,* and *sahasrara,* all of which are above the ajna chakra. All ten chakras are also centers of consciousness and they function like gates. If the gates are open, the pranic forces traveling through the *nadis* can leave the body through them. But at the time of death nine of the ten gates are shut. Our karmas play a crucial role in this, influencing the blocking and unblocking of our energy channels until only the gate through which the prana will finally exit remains open; the unconscious mind and the soul will leave by that same gate.

The relationship between prana and the mind (which includes the senses) is like the relationship between a queen bee and the workers. The workers swarm around the queen; if she leaves the hive, they follow. In the same way, the mind and senses follow the prana as it abandons the *nadis* and their corresponding limbs and organs; they exit the body by the gate through which the queen departed.

Those who lack nonattachment and those who are not fully established in a systematic and authentic spiritual practice are totally at the mercy of their karmas. And since these karmas are contaminated by attachment and a host of other emotions such as desire, fear, hatred, jealousy, and greed, the pranic forces and consciousness are naturally inclined to move toward the lower chakras at the time of death. If we do not understand how karma binds us to the body and how the pranic forces keep the body alive, we are terrified in the face of death. We refuse to leave voluntarily when the messengers of the king of death arrive—but nature kicks us out anyway. It is too late to choose a desirable gate, and we are swept into the unknown.

When the pranic force is gone, the body is lifeless and the afterlife journey begins. We arrive at the river of the mind. Its name is *Vaitarani,* literally "that which can be crossed only by skillful swimmers," for this river is the repository of our karmas, and its crossing is an inner journey. We cannot escape the contents of our mind during this journey. Problems and worries that entangled us during our lifetime ensnare us even more completely now, because in life we had family, friends, teachers, therapists, and—most importantly—our own conscious mind and intellect to help us manage our problems. Now all of these are gone and we are alone with the contents of our unconscious.

Furthermore, while we were residents of the earthly plane, events and experiences took place in sequence—we perceived and experienced only one thing at a time. But the unconscious mind does not follow the laws of time, space, and causation, and we are engulfed by it. Anger, hatred, jealousy, greed, attachment, desire, attraction, repulsion, kindness, cruelty, compassion, self-respect, guilt, and a host of other emotions assail us simultaneously with no discernible cause and in no detectable order. We sink, float, get caught in the current, confront a crocodile, swim easily for a while, inhale contaminated water, or get a push from a friendly dolphin in what seems to be a completely random and chaotic fashion.

The messengers of the king of death are neutral; they understand the law of karma and operate in perfect conformity with it. They drop us at the exact crossing point of the river where we belong. One section of the river is the repository of our active virtuous deeds; that is where the special cows reside. If we are fortunate enough to be deposited there, these intelligent and expert swimmers offer us their tails and pull us across the river. (The Sanskrit word for "cow" is *go*—which is also the word for "senses" and "ray of light.") These cows are charity, selfless service, self-restraint, and spiritual practices that remove the darkness of ignorance. They come to the rescue of those who have risen above their sense cravings as well as those who have been touched by spiritual light and thus have enlightened their inner world. In such cases they come forward and pull us safely to the other shore of the river of mind.

On the other hand, if our mind has been complicated and confused and we have thereby accumulated complicated and confused samskaras, we are deposited at a crossing point where we will confront and struggle with our samskaras. But sooner or later, comfortably or painfully, we arrive at the other shore, having gained some kind of understanding about ourselves. Now another struggle ensues, this one marked by denial and acceptance, guilt and consolation. While it is going on, we see all of our deeds and acknowledge their consequences as well as our responsibility for them. Now we see ourselves clearly; there is no escape from whatever we are.

Next we arrive at the capital city of the king of death. This is *Samyamani Puri,* the city of the inner controller—conscience. And here we meet the king's bookkeeper, Chitra Gupta. *Chitra* means "picture" or "reflection of various forms"; *gupta* means "hidden or mysterious." Thus Chitra Gupta is the voice of our heart, the one who resides hidden in all the forms and shapes we assume throughout life, the one who witnesses our thoughts, speech, and actions. Nothing escapes death's bookkeeper. Since we have by now acknowledged our deeds, their consequences, and our responsibility for them, Chitra Gupta simply confirms this recognition and assigns us either to heaven or to hell on the basis of our karmas.

But if we managed to perfect the art of killing our conscience while we were alive, ignoring the voice of our heart and learning to live comfortably with self-deception, the subtle impressions of this self-deception will cause us to argue with our conscience. If that happens, the bookkeeper brings us to the court of the king of death, Yamaraja, the representative of the immortal within us. He is the foremost teacher and the guru of Nachiketa (the fully prepared student who is totally dedicated to acquiring spiritual knowledge). Yamaraja is at once the kindest and also the most wrathful of beings. His brilliance eclipses a billion suns, and in the face of this dazzling light, truth alone can stand. Our self-deception vanishes and we are bound to go to our rightful place.

Predicting the Destination

Our karmas are the sole vehicle for this journey to heaven or hell, and if we knew what our karmas were, we could predict our destination. The problem is that we cannot grasp the complexity of our karmas with the limited mind and intellect presently at our disposal. And even if we could know all of our karmas, the story of Jaigishavya in chapter two makes it clear that even accomplished yogis can be overwhelmed if they experience all of the infinite number of samskaras deposited in their mind-field. The texts of yoga tell us that it is impossible for anyone other than the omniscient Divine Being to know all of them.

The flow of prana during the time of death is regulated by the forces of our karma. This determines the particular gate through which the pranic force departs, and this in turn shapes the journey that follows. We can make some predictions about the destination of the departed soul, the scriptures tell us, by observing the movement of prana and the precise time it leaves the body.

According to the Bhagavad Gita, all unliberated souls must

follow one of two paths after death: *deva yana* or *pitri yana*, the path of the gods or the path of the ancestors. The path of the gods is bathed in light; the path of the ancestors is shrouded in smoke. The path of the gods is open in the six-month interval between the spring and autumn equinoxes; the path of the ancestors is open the remaining six months. The broad and simple rule is that those who die between the spring and autumn equinoxes go to the realm of the gods, and those who die during the other half of the year go to the realm of the ancestors. Within this broad arrangement, there are more precise times connected to the path of gods or the path of the ancestors. For example, those who die in the daytime go to the realm of the gods, and those who die at night go to the realm of the ancestors.

The yogic interpretation of this is that the six-month period following the spring equinox corresponds to the dominance of solar energy in our body, and this is indicated by the flow of breath through the right nostril *(pingala nadi);* the six-month period following the autumn equinox corresponds to the dominance of lunar energy, indicated by the flow of the breath through the left nostril *(ida nadi).* Accomplished yogis who can leave their bodies at will often do so during twilight when the breath is flowing equally in both nostrils, and prana is likewise flowing through both nostrils. At this time, day and night, sun and moon, are wed, and a yogi leaving the body then goes neither to heaven nor to hell, but transcends both. Regardless of the time of day, however, accomplished yogis can, if they wish, create the atmosphere of twilight within their own body by opening *sushumna nadi* and leaving the body while this *nadi* is active.

The gate through which the prana leaves the body is

another indication of the soul's destination. According to a famous yogic text, *Saundaryalahari,* the two lowest chakras—the *muladhara* and the *svadhishthana*—are connected to the realms of blind darkness and darkness, respectively. The prana of an unliberated soul leaves the body from one of these two chakras and goes to the realm of darkness. Those who leave the body through the *manipura* chakra (the navel center) go to the realm of shining beings *(deva loka)* and are reborn again after enjoying celestial pleasures.

Those who leave their body from any of the chakras above the *manipura* chakra are free from illusion (including the illusion of heaven and hell) and are reborn only if they choose. Hundreds of *nadis* meet at the *anahata* chakra (the heart center). In most of us, these have become entangled and knotted, but they can be disentangled with the help of meditation, contemplation, prayer, selfless service, acts of charity, the blessings of the saints, and God's grace. When that has happened, energy flows freely through all the *nadis* at the heart center, and prana exits from this chakra at the time of death. Following the prana, consciousness leaves the body by the same gate and reaches the realm of the Divine, which transcends both heaven and hell (*Katha Upanishad* 2:3:14–18).

The Freedom to Reap the Fruit of Our Karmas

How much freedom of choice do we have in deciding when and how we die and where we go after death? Both the scriptures and the sages tell us that humans have a great degree of freedom in this regard. We are the only species that can, through our actions, create new karmas and erase old ones.

Nature has given us the ability to think, decide, plan, and execute our plans. No other species has this privilege to the extent that we do. That is why we are the only species classified as *karma yonis*—beings who can reap the fruits of their actions.

According to the scriptures, all living beings fall into one of three categories: *divya yonis, bhoga yonis,* or *karma yonis.* Divya yonis are beings who inhabit a body made of pure light, rather than a material body. This is a subtle body, and it is the locus for their consciousness, which consists of the mind and senses. Divya yonis perceive, feel, and experience just as we do. They perform actions, but their actions do not bear any fruit. The scriptures tell us that these so-called celestial beings were once humans who accumulated uplifting samskaras through good works and spiritual practices. However, because they had little knowledge, they could neither disidentify themselves from their good deeds nor surrender them to the Divine. Their good actions were motivated by their expectations of reward, and so they have been rewarded with a celestial body and heavenly pleasures.

But divya yonis do not have the privilege of finding the purpose of life or even the privilege of searching for it—they lack the ability and the resources to undertake spiritually illuminating practices. They live on their storehouse of good karmas, which as humans they could have reinvested for a higher purpose: enlightenment and freedom from the cycle of birth and death. Thus by inhabiting a celestial body they actually go backward in their spiritual evolution. When the karmas that brought them their body of light are exhausted, they return to the earthly plane to find the meaning and purpose of life.

The second species of living beings, bhoga yonis, have little or no freedom to change their circumstances or to escape from them. Species belonging to this class have a limited capacity to sense and feel. Nature gives them some small ability to experience pleasure, but their consciousness is mainly occupied with satisfying their primitive urges: hunger, sleep, sex, and self-preservation. Their bodies are equipped with underdeveloped brains and nervous systems; the sensory organs that enable them to survive and procreate are the only senses that are well developed.

Nothing a bhoga yoni does in the course of completing its life cycle creates karma. A lion, for example, does not incur any karma by killing a human. Just as the celestial beings exhaust their karmas by enjoying extraterrestrial pleasures, bhoga yonis exhaust their karmas simply by completing their life cycle in the manner dictated by nature. At the time of death they are not affected by the subtle impressions of their actions, because their actions are guided by instinct, and instinct is governed by nature. The barely evolved intelligence and lack of ego of these beings prevents them from identifying with their actions, so they experience neither shame nor guilt. Except for the instinct to cling to life, their consciousness is not cluttered by desire, attachment, or a sense of guilt and regret at the time of death.

Some scriptures say that bhoga yonis are those who did not exercise their power of intelligence and discrimination when they were human. They accumulated degrading samskaras by performing base actions which, due to their ignorance, they could neither purify nor surrender. But these scriptures warn us that adopting a self-righteous or punitive attitude toward this category of beings is itself a base action, one that generates the same kind of karma that leads to birth as a bhoga yoni. For example, feeling that a stray cat's pain and misery is the result of its karma, and hence feeling indifference toward the cat's wretched state, creates a base karma that can pull us down to a similar miserable state.

The third category of beings, that of karma yonis, is gifted with a high level of intelligence, organized mental faculties, and a body composed of an efficient brain, nervous system, and sensory organs. Like bhoga yonis, we humans are influenced by the four instinctual urges of food, sleep, sex, and the desire for self-preservation, but our knowledge and power of discrimination prevent us from being completely motivated by our instincts. Our extraordinary gifts bring with them greater responsibility—we can and do reap the fruit of our actions.

Although, with rare exceptions, humans lack perfect freedom of choice, if we make the best use of the freedom we do have, we can eventually extricate ourselves from the bondage of karma. The efficient tools granted us by nature enable us to distinguish right from wrong and to differentiate the unreal from the real. We have the ability to make conscious decisions, verify their validity in the light of reason, and act on them. We also have the privilege of drawing on the vast knowledge and experiences of all those who have come before us. Therefore, unlike diyva yonis and bhoga yonis, who exist for the sole purpose of exhausting the karmas which brought them to these states in the first place, the purpose of life as a karma yoni is to perform actions which destroy, or at least loosen, previous karmic bonds and to gain direct experience of the immortal self. This opportunity comes only with a human birth.

Performing Good Karmas

Because it is through our actions that we become the creators of our destiny, we must be vigilant about what we do. The law of karma is so complex it is unlikely that we will ever understand exactly which karma or group of karmas causes us to be born as a sage, a queen, a dog, a caterpillar, or a plant. But whether we understand it or not, destiny is the result of our karmas. We plant seeds which eventually sprout, grow, blossom, and bear fruit. We are not entirely aware of the dynamics of this process, yet the process goes on. The same force that makes an apple seed grow into a tree that bears apples rather than coconuts, peaches, or walnuts also ensures that the karmic seeds we plant eventually bear the proper fruit.

We have seen that our previous karmas keep us from having perfect freedom of choice, yet the freedom we do have is sufficient to make us the creators of our destiny. The doctrine of karma is not fatalistic. On the contrary, it proclaims that God or divine providence helps those who help themselves. If we use our present level of freedom with full determination and faith, nature begins to grant us a wider range of freedom. That is how we evolve spiritually. By listening to our inner voice and consulting scriptures and saints to confirm its validity, we can arrive at the right understanding of our actions.

Then, if we perform our present actions selflessly, lovingly, and skillfully we attenuate old unwholesome karmas and at the same time generate new, positive, and uplifting karmas. This is karma yoga, selfless service. And once we begin restructuring our destiny by following the path of karma yoga, divine providence comes to our aid in one form or another.

Actions performed on the path of karma yoga cannot of course change the course of destiny in our present life—destiny has already determined our birth, longevity, and other aspects of our fate. But such actions can minimize the influence of the secondary strands of our destiny, and by doing so they can prevent future misery.

The path of karma yoga is the foundation for all other paths. Selfless service purifies the way of the soul, and without such purification our mind and heart remain caught in worldly concerns. Regardless of which spiritual path we ultimately follow, we cannot bypass karma yoga—it helps us earn virtues, which in turn draw God's grace toward us in the form of right thinking *(vichara)* and meeting wise people *(satsanga)* at the crucial moments in life.

The scriptures tell us that a master appears when a student is prepared. Selfless service is the means of preparation. It begins to transform the mind's tendency to identify itself solely with the material world into a tendency to be attracted to the more subtle realms of existence. Thus the scriptures ask, "How can those who have not performed good karmas either meditate on thee or even acknowledge thee, O Divine Mother?" *(Saundaryalahari* 1)

Creating Spiritually Powerful Samskaras

Creating good karmas helps lay the groundwork, but by itself karma yoga is a long and drawn-out way of freeing ourselves from the bondage of karma. Even the noblest act of nonviolence and compassion involves some degree of pain to someone, somewhere—there is no action perfectly devoid of negative karmic effects. No matter how skillfully and wisely we perform our actions while living in the world, they are bound to be contaminated to some degree. Complete freedom from the bondage of karma involves stepping out of the realm of karma—including the practice of karma yoga.

We do this through meditation. The *Yoga Sutra* tells us that only samskaras created in this way do not create further bondage. And in the highest state of samadhi, even the samskara of meditation vanishes completely. The scriptures advise us to use the path of selfless service as a stepping-stone but to avoid becoming attached to the stepping-stone. We must be vigilant. While dedicating ourselves to the path of service, we must also explore one of the paths that leads directly to the final destination. The paths of meditation, knowledge, and devotion are such paths. Each of these, when pursued with diligence, is like a keen sword which cuts asunder all the ropes of karma, or like a fire which burns them.

A spiritual discipline becomes even more powerful and effective when it is accompanied by faith, enthusiasm, retentive power, one-pointedness, and intuitive wisdom (*Yoga Sutra* 1:20–21). And if we commit ourselves to an intense spiritual practice, we will draw closer to the goal even faster. Intensity makes a spiritual discipline shine.

When our practice is intense we become so absorbed in it that nothing else matters anymore. When we pour our entire mind and heart into our practice with true fervor, all else vanishes, even our concern about whether or not the practice will yield the desired result. The samskaras created by such an intensity are more potent than the samskaras created by our normal activities, and in the face of such powerful spiritual samskaras, the samskaras of other actions—regardless of how influential they had been previously—lose their potency.

The other way of creating powerful spiritual samskaras is to surrender ourselves to God (*Yoga Sutra* 1:23). Samskaras created in this way will also outshine all others. But the path of surrender is not easy. In fact it is actually more demanding and difficult than the path of intense practice, requiring as it does whole-hearted devotion to, and meditation on, God.

The yogis tell us that intense practice or complete surrender creates the deepest grooves in the mind-field, and the resulting samskaras therefore occupy the mind at the time of death. Then, at the moment of death, when the mind becomes free from memories, anxieties, fears, desires, attachments, and every other thought or emotion, the pranic forces are channeled toward the chakra which had been the focal point of practice, and leave the body from that center. For example, the prana and unconscious mind of a *bhakti* yogi who always meditates at the heart center exits through the heart center.

Restarting the Journey

The purpose of life is to realize our true self—that which is divine and one with the universal self. If we have accomplished this, we are reabsorbed into the immortal self at the time of death and are totally free from the journey after life.

If we have committed ourselves to surrender or to an intense practice but have not reached perfect realization when death arrives, we still leave the body in a glorious way. Love for the practice will have destroyed our interest in both heaven and hell and freed us from the emotions which usually bind us to our friends and enemies. We have no need to experience the pleasures of heaven or the pains of hell. Our *chitta* (unconscious) is absorbed in its broader counterpart, prakriti (primordial nature), which becomes the custodian of our unconscious.

Just as nature ensures that an apple seed produces only apples, nature makes sure that we are born at the right time, in the right place, and to the right family. In the Bhagavad Gita (6:37–45) Lord Krishna tells Arjuna, "A yogi committed to intense practice who dies before completing the practice is born into a family of resourceful yogis." The *Yoga Sutra* (1:19) calls such people *bhava pratyaya* yogis—that is, yogis who inherit the knowledge and experience of yoga by birth. They are also known as *videhas* or *prakriti layas*—that is, those who remain absorbed in prakriti until their rebirth.

In the subtle realm, appropriate parents attract us if we are among this fortunate few, and we attract them. Thus we are born into a family that is equipped to provide the resources we need to continue our journey as accomplished yogis. For example, if we are a *videha* or a *prakriti laya* we may be born to a father who possesses a great deal of knowledge and is well versed in the scriptures. His company and his library become a source of inspiration. Our mother's selflessness and the tenderness of her love opens our heart. Learned teachers and wise people visit the family periodically, offering unconditional love and guidance, and we resume or journey at the point where it was interrupted by death.

Another possibility is that the opportunity to restart our journey may emerge in a mysterious, dramatic, or even unpleasant manner. For example, our parents may die while we are still children. Deprived of love and care, a saint may come along and adopt us, transforming our grief and feelings of abandonment into love for God and surrender. Raised thus in a yogic manner, by the time we are adolescents we are already well along on the path.

In any case, those who dedicate their life to an intense practice but die before completing it leave their body with peace of mind. They are not confronted by death's bookkeeper. Like a compassionate mother, nature becomes their custodian. Such people leave the world gracefully, and with the help of nature's intelligence reenter the world gracefully.

Those of us who are on a less intense path accumulate spiritual samskaras of a milder potency, along with other karmas and their samskaras. We come to this world with a host of positive and negative karmas and live a life composed of pleasant and unpleasant experiences; we have both mundane and spiritual desires, and hence ride the roller coaster of success and failure, honor and insult, pleasure and pain. Occasionally we see the inner light, and then lose it again. Thus we experience some commotion at the time of death. We must cross the river of mind, sort out our unresolved issues, face our conscience, and stay awhile in heaven or hell before being born once more.

In this way we return exactly as we left: before death we were engulfed by our unconscious, and we regain consciousness again only after we are born. Although we experience pleasure and pain in the period between death and birth, this interlude remains unknown to us. When we are reborn, we have to learn everything again because we have lost all the knowledge we had gathered through the senses and the conscious mind. However, the subtle impressions of all this information are stored in the unconscious mind, so it is relatively easy to relearn it all provided we are born in the right environment with the right resources. At some point we will again become interested in spiritual practices, although half-heartedly, and we will once again go back and forth between worldly and spiritual concerns.

The Fruit of Intense Practice

There are many stories of miraculous transformations involving those who had been dedicated to an intense practice in a previous life. These people seem to acquire great spiritual wisdom with minimal effort in this lifetime, and we wonder why, failing to comprehend the intense effort they have put into their sadhana in the past. Because they seem to achieve great success with little effort, we say they are blessed. We attribute their present success to God's grace alone. The truth is that such people have reincarnated rather than being reborn. These are the *videhas* and *prakriti layas*.

Reincarnation is the fruit of intense practice. Yoga scriptures make a clear distinction between rebirth *(punar janma)* and reincarnation *(avatara)*. *Punar janma* literally means "again birth," and carries a connotation of weariness. *Avatara* means "to descend."

Then there are the fortunate few who, after dedicating themselves to intense practice, achieve the goal: the realization of the self at every level. Through their practice and God's grace, they unveil the mystery of the body, pranic forces, mind, samskaras, and consciousness, as well as the relationship between individual and universal consciousness. This enables them to experience the fact that although they have a body and a mind, they are nevertheless totally separate from either their body or their mind. Rising above both, they experience their oneness with the Supreme. And as this knowledge dawns, the darkness of ignorance, egoism, attachment, aversion, and fear of death totally vanishes. Then the unconscious mind can no longer bind the soul to the body.

If such adepts continue to maintain a body, they do so not because the force of karma demands it—in their case, there are no karmas left—but because they are one with the Divine and are acting out of that oneness. They are called *apta kamas*—adepts whose every desire is fulfilled and who are under no obligation to perform any action of any kind. Whatever actions they now engage in bear no fruit for them; such actions as they do choose to perform are freely rendered solely for the benefit of others.

Such adepts are immortal—death cannot touch them, because death applies only to those who have karmas. They are free from desire, attachment, fear, and any sense of loss or gain, so it makes no difference to them whether they have a body or not. When the body no longer serves a purpose they cast it off, just as we ordinary people take off our clothes. They choose the exact method of casting off the body, and voluntarily return its physical elements to nature. Following the instructions of such an adept, prana leaves the body in the exact manner that the adept orders it to leave. The gross elements of the body return to dust, the pranas are reabsorbed into the cosmic life-force, and the mind into prakriti.

These *apta kamas* are no longer part of the cycle of rebirth or reincarnation. Whenever, under the will of the Divine, they are inspired to return to this world, they emerge through divine birth, in a mysterious process beyond both rebirth and reincarnation known as *divya janma* (divine birth). Because we do not comprehend the fact that someone can enter this world without being born, we sometimes call such a phenomenon "immaculate birth," even though birth in the sense that we understand it is not involved. A more accurate term for it is "emergence."

Yoga scriptures explain the entire dynamics of divine emergence systematically. They show, for example, how an adept can leave the body they have been inhabiting and enter one that has been abandoned by its original inhabitant—a technique known as *parakaya pravesha* (*Yoga Sutra* 3:37). In other instances, they tell us that a yogi can create a body solely from the powers of the mind. And the mind itself is created by the sheer force of the yogi's *asmita*, "I-am-ness" (*Yoga Sutra* 4:4–6). But before we discuss the dynamics of death, birth, reincarnation, and divine birth, we must first determine the extent to which the law of karma governs the process of death, birth, and reincarnation, and at what point this law no longer applies. We will do this by analyzing the subtle nature and function of rebirth, reincarnation, and divine emergence.

CHAPTER SEVEN

THE RETURN OF THE SOUL

JIVA IS THE SANSKRIT WORD for the individual soul. Caught in the endless cycle of birth and death, the jiva must play different roles in different lifetimes, and therefore requires garments of different shapes and sizes. Each of our bodies is a different garment for jiva. After completing one role, the individual soul must take off its costume and don one that suits its next role. And just as costumes are manufactured in the external world, the body that clothes the individual soul is generated by nature.

If this body is indeed a garment we put on, then why is it we don't remember that we did this? The answer is to be found in scriptures such as the *Yoga Vasishtha,* the Bhagavad Gita, the *Yoga Sutra,* the *Katha Upanishad,* and the *Garbha Upanishad,* which tell us that those who fall asleep before dying remain asleep when they are being reborn. (In this context, "sleep" means "lack of conscious awareness.") In other words, those who die unconsciously remain unaware of their birth. According to the scriptures, however, birth has nothing to do with conception or delivery. Birth takes place the moment we identify ourselves with a particular body, and this is why sages and yogic adepts are never born even when they inhabit a body: they never identify themselves with that body.

As we saw in the previous chapter, under most circumstances death is accompanied by confusion and chaos. When prana departs, the body, brain, and conscious mind become lifeless, and the jiva is left with the unconscious mind. That is the vehicle with which it leaves the body. This kind of death can be compared to a blind man trying to get out of an unfamiliar house. Because of the confusion caused by our desires and attachments, we do not even know through which door we are leaving.

In the interval after death we are in the realm of our unconscious, experiencing pain or pleasure until the strongest among the subtle impressions of our karmas gathers momentum and pushes us in the direction of rebirth. These powerful samskaras (called *vasanas*) stir the unconscious, motivating us to grope around for a body. But we are in such a deep sleep that we are not even aware of this stirring, although we feel it on an unconscious level.

This unconscious stirring is so strong that we cannot resist it. Here again nature takes a hand. Making sure we find a body that meets the needs of our vasanas, nature brings us to parents who have vasanas similar to ours. The vasanas from both sides—ours, and our parents'—attract each other. Just being in the proximity of such a body offers a sense of security to our unconscious mind. The pranic forces reemerge from nature and enter the body, giving it life. And following the trail of prana, riding the vehicle of the unconscious mind, the individual soul (jiva) enters the fetus.

The formation of the brain, the seat of the conscious mind,

is a crucial stage in pregnancy. According to the *Garbha Upanishad,* when that has happened the soul has the tools to think and feel. In a sense it has entered the world, although it is still living in the confines of the mother's womb. Even so, the unconscious mind of the fetus is quite active, even more so than the unconscious mind of children and adults. This is because the conscious mind of a fetus has no opportunity to occupy itself with sensory diversions, and so experiences the unconscious vividly and intensely.

During the period between death and conception, the soul has been encapsulated in the unconscious. Even though it had been experiencing pain and pleasure, it had no conscious experience of this. It did not even know where it was. But now with the development of the nervous system, brain, and conscious mind, memories have returned.

The jiva now knows that it is being reborn. It remembers its previous lives and clearly knows the reason for being born into this particular species under these particular conditions. It remembers how painful it is to die and to be born. Its tender senses and mind are bombarded by the racket in its mother's body and jolted by her emotions. The primitive instinct of hunger has also returned, and in an attempt to cope with it, the fetus begins to suck its own toes or thumbs.

The jiva now realizes what a great loss it has been to die without attaining the goal of life, and it does not want to make that mistake again. Regretting the waste of its previous lives, it prays to the Divine Being, "O God, I have been traveling from one species to another for thousands of lifetimes. I have suckled different breasts and eaten different kinds of food only to be born and only to die. I cannot see a way out of this ocean of pain and misery. I performed good and bad actions, telling

myself that it was my duty and I was doing it for my loved
ones. Today I am suffering alone from the pain of those
scorching actions. O Lord, help me get out of this place. This
time I promise I will embrace you alone and serve only you."
(*Garbha Upanishad,* 4)

Occupying itself with these thoughts, feelings, and prayers,
the jiva completes the period of gestation. But when the infant
emerges from the womb, it touches a pranic force known as
vaishnava prana, which wipes away all memories. The amnesia
is so total that the infant does not even remember its birth.
The thoughts and feelings it had in the womb, its prayers—
everything—vanishes, and the infant's conscious mind is like
a clean slate. The baby must relearn everything by means of
its environment, its parents, and its teachers, and later on,
through self-study and personal experience.

This description of the soul's journey from death to birth is
disheartening. We often feel as if the forces of time, nature,
karma, or destiny are cruel, especially when we hear how
vaishnava prana erases our memory at the time of birth, taking
with it the privilege of using the knowledge and lessons we
had received in our previous lives. People in ancient times
also wanted to know why vaishnava prana erases our memory,
rendering moot the prayers and resolutions we made during
the gestation period. The following story, briefly mentioned
in several Puranas and told in elaborate detail in the *Skanda
Purana,* clarifies these issues.

———

Late one morning, after completing his practice on a bank
of the Ganges, the sage Vyasa was returning to his ashram
when he noticed a caterpillar on the roadside. It seemed to be
disoriented and in a great hurry to cross the road. Nothing was

chasing it and it did not seem to be looking for food, but the kind sage sensed an intense fear in the creature and stopped for a moment to see if there was anything he could do to help. The sage had the capacity to communicate with all species in creation, so he asked the caterpillar why he was frightened and where he was going in such a rush. While continuing to crawl as fast as he could, the caterpillar replied, "I have no time to waste. If I don't cross this road and reach safety on the other side, I'll be killed. And you'd better get off the road too, you giant caterpillar."

"How do you think you are going to be killed and why do you think you will be safe on the other side of the road?" the sage inquired.

The caterpillar replied, "Don't you hear the deafening sound of drums and trumpets? Can't you hear the elephants and horses? A royal procession is on its way and we will be squashed if we stay on the road."

Hearing this, Vyasa's heart melted with compassion, and he made a firm decision to protect and guide the creature, not only in this lifetime but also in all the lives to come until it attained final liberation. "Don't worry," he said. "I am not a giant caterpillar, but Vyasa. I will protect you. But first tell me, what is so pleasant about being a caterpillar that you do not want to die?"

Although the caterpillar could not understand what Vyasa meant, the sage's mere presence gave it a sense of security and safety. The creature's instinct told it that Vyasa would do it no harm. So it stopped its frantic race across the road and answered, "Is there anyone who is not afraid of dying? The pain that precedes and accompanies death lasts forever. And once I die I will lose everything—the lovely green grass, and my friends and loved ones."

At that, the caterpillar curled up and began to sob. Consoling the creature, Vyasa said, "Don't worry. I'll protect you from being crushed by the royal procession. But death is inevitable; sooner or later, everyone dies. Real safety comes from knowing the cause of birth and death and removing it once and for all. With my yogic power, I will grant you the memory of your previous lives, as far back as your last human birth. Then tell me the story of your transmigration."

The caterpillar instantly gained the memories of several lifetimes and began its story.

"Born in a brahmin family, I was a highly educated and respected teacher," the caterpillar said. "I had a large following. People were enchanted by my discourses, and I was amused by their gullibility. I was quite arrogant, even as a student. I always thought my teachers slow and dull-witted. I was proud of myself and of the fact that within a matter of months I could master scriptures which my teachers had learned only after several years of intense study. My teachers knew I was arrogant, egotistical, and even disrespectful to them, but they always treated me gently and lovingly. I interpreted their treatment as weakness and timidity. This attitude became the leading trait of my personality.

"Later on, when I became a teacher myself, I was convinced that everyone else in the world was dull-witted. I never practiced the philosophy I taught, and still I was considered an expert teacher. This made me feel that the systems of philosophy and spirituality were nothing but intellectual theories. And because my intellectual knowledge did not transform me, I thought that all other learned people were just like me. I concluded that everyone in the past and the present had been teaching for the sake of livelihood, pretending to be highly evolved spiritually. I believed that everyone in the world was a hypocrite, and therefore there was nothing wrong with my being a hypocrite too.

"I taught others to be selfless and God-minded. I inspired them to practice purity, simplicity, nonpossessiveness, and contentment. I pretended that I myself practiced all these virtues, but I did not. In fact, when I was by myself I used to laugh at those who believed in me and followed me with such trust. I lived a luxurious life, enjoying wine, women, and sumptuous food.

"Occasionally a voice came from within telling me I was not on the right path, but I suppressed it with the force of my reason. I was so preoccupied with pleasures that I never realized there was a constant war going on in my inner world.

"To cut the story short: I eventually became old and sick. And finally, when I was on my deathbed I started seeing myself more clearly than I had during my youth. But it was too late. At that point my crafty intellect told me to identify myself as a *jnani* yogi [an aspirant on the path of knowledge] so that I could throw all my actions into the fire of knowledge. But a voice from within said, 'You self-proclaimed wise man, the scriptures are not to be distorted for your convenience.'

"I was filled with remorse at the time of death and so I swam the river of my mind very painfully. It seemed like eons before I reached the other shore—the point of conclusion, where I clearly saw the sum of my self and the actions performed by me in that lifetime. My conscience, the bookkeeper, told me that I had been a chameleon. So I was next born as a chameleon and in that life I had to change my color to camouflage myself in order to catch my prey, or safely lift a dewdrop from a blade of grass to quench my thirst. Later I was born as an elephant, but despite my strength and intelligence I was controlled by a mahout who sat on my neck and forced me to work at trident-point. I also remember being a snake, a donkey, and many other creatures.

"Each time I was between births I remembered the reason for being trapped in the body of such a species and I prayed to God to help me. I resolved not to commit the mistake of killing my conscience as I had in my human birth, but always right after being born I found myself totally occupied with the urges of hunger, sleep, procreation, and self-preservation, and this caused me to forget the prayers and the resolutions I had made. Even now as a caterpillar I have had no idea of anything other than these urges. Am I again going to lose these memories, which I have received through your grace?

"The memory of myself as a human forces me to ask you some questions: Who or what caused me to be born as a chameleon, elephant, or caterpillar: my own conscience, God, nature, destiny? Why did I remember about myself, my actions, and their consequences while I was between births, and why did I forget afterwards? Is this the case with everybody, or only with me?"

Vyasa replied, "In truth it is your own conscience that has directed you to go through the cycle of birth and death, assuming different bodies. Conscience has its source in the Atman, the universal self. Atman abides in you. It is the supreme truth, and conscience is its light. The light of conscience sees no distinction between you and those whom you love or hate, because conscience is a thread that runs throughout nature, God, and destiny. In every circumstance you are accompanied by your conscience, and all actions—physical, verbal, or mental—are witnessed by it. Therefore conscience is called 'the eye of God,' and it is through your conscience that you reward or punish yourself. Just as a patch of cloud is smaller than the sun and yet can veil it to human sight, the forces of mind, intellect, reason, and logic veil this inner light. But sooner or later it shines forth.

"The light of conscience clearly told you that you had been a chameleon, so you became a chameleon. And by becoming a chameleon you discharged the karmas you gathered through your hypocritical deeds as a human. But had you not forgotten that you had been human, you would not have been happy as a chameleon, an elephant, a snake, a donkey, or any of the other bodies you assumed; you would have been miserable in those forms. The feelings of shame, regret, guilt, and self-condemnation would have been intense when you met and recognized the people you misled during that lifetime and they recognized you! By forgetting everything, you completed the normal course of life with relative ease. Had you remembered, you would have brooded about your past. But because you were ignorant, you had to deal only with your current circumstances.

"Those who are not fully established in the principle of *vairagya* [nonattachment] are always victims of their thoughts, memories, and emotions. Realizing this, nature throws a blanket of forgetfulness over our mind, thus granting us freedom from memories and their attendant anxieties. Nature does this with the help of vaishnava prana."

"But by doing so, vaishnava prana also deleted the lesson I had learned," the caterpillar argued.

The sage replied, "You did not learn any lesson. You simply became the victim of the consequences of your actions. What you think of as a lesson was nothing more than a momentary emotional outburst. And even that came very late. Learning a lesson requires a properly organized mind, a sharpened intellect, and a strong power of determination—conditions available only in human life. When you lived in the body of a chameleon, snake, or caterpillar you had no tools with which to correct your actions or to clean up the mess you created as a human.

"Vaishnava prana, which erases all memories before birth, is an act of grace; it erases not only your memory but the memories of all those affected by your actions. Because they too lack memory, they do not hold you responsible for your actions, nor do they feel animosity toward you. In this manner, vaishnava prana cleans up the mess and grants you freedom from the animosity, revenge, and remorse which would otherwise follow you from life to life.

"Through my yogic power, you remembered only your past, not the past of those who were associated with you when you were human. Furthermore, you remembered yourself and the consequences of your actions only up to this moment, not beyond. Now let me reveal a further portion of your story to you.

"One day, when you were a famous teacher, you led a procession riding on the back of an elephant. Your followers joined you, putting on an impressive show. Today as a caterpillar you are afraid of being crushed by those whose honor and dignity you yourself crushed. By the grace of vaishnava prana they do not remember you, nor do you remember them. And yet nature has granted you the opportunity to pay off your karma."

"It makes sense that while living in the body of a less evolved species we forget about our human life and its events," the caterpillar humbly replied. "But these memories can act as a beacon when we are reborn as a human. So why is it necessary for vaishnava prana, which is an active manifestation of grace, to wipe out memories?"

Vyasa replied, "Humans have a greater sense of self-identity and possessiveness than other species. The attachment, desire, hatred, jealousy, greed, animosity, friendship, love, cruelty, sympathy, and insensitivity they harbor in their present lives make their lives complicated enough. If memories of past lives brought more of these same thoughts, feelings, and sentiments forward, how would humans conduct their lives? How, for example, could a man raise his child lovingly if he knew that this same child had murdered him in a past lifetime?

"Now that you know your own personal story, which unveils just a fraction of the complex dynamics of karma and its effect on your deaths and rebirths, tell me, do you want me to put you on the other side of the road?"

The caterpillar replied, "Sir, although I am still afraid of death, I am more concerned about permanent safety. I surrender myself to you. Please, you decide."

"I will leave you on the road," Vyasa replied. "By using your instincts as a caterpillar and your physical ability, try to crawl in the direction which seems safest to you as fast as you can. If destiny dictates that you remain alive, you will reach safety.

"Don't be afraid of dying. With my blessings, from now on you will have no pain either during the time of death or at birth. You will retain the memory of the lifetimes you have recalled today, and you will also have knowledge of all your lifetimes yet to come until you attain final liberation. However, after death you will lose your memory for a moment, and then regain it after destiny has placed you in the body in which you are to be born next.

"Your next human birth will be your last. In this birth you will enlighten an ardent seeker, Nanda Bhadra, and soon after that you will attain freedom from the cycle of birth and death."

The caterpillar's story gives us some idea of why we die and are reborn. The opportunity for self-transformation and for climbing the ladder of spiritual evolution is found only in human life. That is why the Upanishads say, "If we can attain self-realization before the destruction of the body, the purpose of life is fulfilled. If not, we remain caught in the cycle of transmigration and continue going from one body to another. That is the greatest loss."

Reincarnation

As we have discussed earlier, those who dedicate themselves to attaining knowledge of the purpose of life, putting their mind and heart into sadhana (spiritual practice), are blessed with a higher form of rebirth, known as reincarnation. Those who die before completing their sadhana reincarnate. Following the law of karma, nature rewards their intense sadhana by placing them in the right family. And even if such souls are reborn in a nonhuman species for some reason, they still retain a higher level of intelligence than their fellow creatures, and perhaps they even retain the memory of their previous lifetimes. The following story from the *Srimad Bhagavatam* will give a sense of the process of reincarnation and the conditions it involves.

There once was a saint named Bharata. Content within, this saint lived in solitude in his ashram near a peaceful stream.

One day a doe who was just about to have a fawn came to drink from this stream; suddenly sensing the presence of a tiger, she made a frantic attempt to leap across the stream—and fell, injuring herself fatally. In her death throes the fawn was born. Bharata, observing these events, was driven by compassion to adopt the newborn deer.

The saint came to love the fawn and raised it as he would his own child. And in his company the fawn lost its natural instincts and became totally dependent on the holy man. But within a few months Bharata fell mortally ill. Although he had mastered the technique of casting off his body at will (thereby avoiding the normal journey after life), he was so worried about what would happen to the fawn that as he died his mind was fully occupied with the deer. His attachment had made him so weak that he failed to remember how to leave his body consciously, so he died as ordinary people do and was reincarnated as a deer.

However, because he still remembered his previous life, Bharata was not caught up in the four primitive urges like other deer—he ate just enough to sustain his body, and had no fear of predators. He had no regrets about being born as a deer, but spent most of his time in contemplation. And with the help of introspection and self-analysis, he came to understand the difference between compassion and sentimentality.

When he realized that his time as a deer was almost finished, he decided to drop his body. He remembered the yogic technique he had mastered as a saint, but he could not use it while he was in the form of a deer. So instead, following the path known as *muni brata,* he undertook the austere practice of fasting until he died.

Next the sage reincarnated as a human. This time he was

blessed with all the means and resources he needed to accomplish the highest goal of life: a body and mind perfectly fit for intense sadhana and an environment that was conducive to this. Circumstances freed him from worldly duties at a very early age, and soon after renouncing the world he became fully established in perfect wisdom. During this lifetime he transcended his body-consciousness through his sadhana, and gaining perfect mastery over all the faculties of mind, he rose above the realms ruled by the laws of karma, destiny, death, and birth.

This story illustrates the dynamics of reincarnation. Bharata was established in wisdom and had almost attained freedom from all his karmas. Then, shortly before he died, he incurred a karma that clouded his mind at the moment of death. He saved the fawn out of sheer kindness, but by identifying himself with this action, he contaminated it, thus compromising its value. Further, his emotional involvement in helping the fawn led him to worry about the fawn's future—he forgot that it was God saving the fawn through him and that he was simply an instrument in the hands of the primordial savior, the Divine Being. Bharata also forgot that the same Divine Being would continue to help the fawn after his death. In the presence of an omnipresent God, no creature is helpless.

Had he been occupied with other, more worldly thoughts and emotions at the time of death he could have been swept up by the messengers of death and stranded at the river of his mind by confusion and commotion. But as it was, his only thought was concern about the deer, so his entire awareness subsided into deer-consciousness. His samskaras of faith, enthusiasm, retentive power, one-pointedness, and intuitive wisdom were so strong that the pranic forces left his body peacefully, and his mind, accompanied by deer-consciousness, was absorbed in nature. Then, to free him from the deer karma, nature placed him in the body of a deer. Once there, mother nature, in her compassion, restored his memory. Thus, although living in a deer's body Bharata was still gifted with the saintly samskaras of his previous life.

According to yoga tradition, this was not a rebirth but a reincarnation, and reincarnated souls retain samskaras to a greater or lesser degree, depending on their level of spiritual achievement in the previous lifetime. The previous knowledge of these highly evolved, incarnated souls manifests more spontaneously than does the knowledge of those who are less evolved. But all such souls are blessed with the opportunity to pick up their journey at the exact place they left off in their previous life—although the form in which that opportunity will manifest cannot be predicted. There are hundreds of such stories centered around the Buddha when, during the process of his spiritual evolution, he incarnated into several species as a bodhisattva.

The story of Bharata also illustrates the fact that even a highly evolved soul may incarnate for a time in nonhuman form. Our human ego would prefer not to believe that it can ever go backward, but if we allow ourselves to be caught in animal behavior and nurture inhuman samskaras, how can we be reborn as human? Even a holy man cannot expect to harvest grapes if he plants poison ivy.

There is also the popular belief that incarnated souls always have a high degree of spiritual wisdom or are very evolved spiritually. This is not always true. A person of strong will and determination may cut asunder most of their karmas, and as a result transcend the ordinary process of death and birth. But such a person may still remain entangled in one or more powerful karmas, causing the soul to incarnate solely to work out those karmas. Most of us have encountered people who are simple, loving, kind, generous, and generally God-minded, yet who are obsessed with one desire—the desire for a child, for example, or the desire to propagate a particular religion or socio-political agenda, or the desire to vanquish an enemy. In such cases the forces generated by willpower, determination, good actions, austerity, prayer, meditation, and so on are all directed toward fulfilling that single goal.

According to the scriptures, the consciousness of such a person is concentrated on that one desire during the time of death. And this one-pointedness inspires nature to place that person in the environment most suitable to fulfilling that desire. Such people incarnate in an atmosphere so intense that their entire energy automatically moves in the direction of their desired goal, as we see in the following story from the *Mahabharata*.

———

Bhishma was a royal prince, an unmatched warrior, and an accomplished yogi. Death, old age, and sickness were at his command. Death could touch him only when Bhishma chose. For a complex set of reasons, he had taken a vow of lifelong celibacy.

There was a long-standing tradition for the princesses of the royal family of Banaras to marry the princes of Bhishma's dynasty, and it was a matter of honor on both sides to maintain this tradition. This practice could be altered only if the princess preferred someone else or if there was no prince of Bhishma's dynasty of marriageable age. But the king of Banaras violated this tradition by inviting princes from different kingdoms to a ceremony in which his daughters would select their own grooms. And as a deliberate insult, the king had excluded the princes of Bhishma's family from the ceremony. Bhishma was so enraged when he heard this that he burst into the ceremony and attacked not only the king of Banaras but the other kings and princes as well. After defeating them all, he marched into the palace and with the utmost courtesy reminded the king's three daughters of the long-standing agreement between the two families. He offered to take them back to his kingdom as wives for his stepbrothers if they had no objections. All three princesses agreed to accompany him home.

When they arrived, two of the sisters expressed delight at the prospect of marrying Bhishma's stepbrothers, but the third, Amba, confessed her love for the prince of Salva. When he heard this, Bhishma immediately had her escorted to the kingdom of Salva with all due ceremony and respect. But the prince, jealous of his honor, refused Amba on the grounds that she had been rejected by Bhishma.

Having nowhere else to go, princess Amba returned to Bhishma and demanded that he marry her. Bhishma reminded her that before inviting the sisters to come with him, he had clearly stated that he was acting not on his own behalf but on behalf of his stepbrothers. He told Amba that she should have told him then that she had already given her heart to someone else. But refusing to listen to reason, Amba continued to argue vehemently that Bhishma must marry her. Bhishma told her that he could never break his vow of celibacy and reminded the princess that when she had told him she loved someone else, he had immediately arranged for her to go to her beloved. By doing this, he had discharged his duty to her.

Amba refused to give up. She put pressure on Bhishma's stepmother and the wise men in the assembly to force him to marry her. She even approached Bhishma's guru, the sage Parashurama, in an attempt to influence him—all to no avail. Furious at being thwarted, Amba then took a vow before the assembly that she would be the cause of Bhishma's death, no matter how many lifetimes it took.

Intent on revenge, she committed herself to an intense practice of austerities and prayer. She was totally one-pointed. Her only goal was to vanquish Bhishma. Decades passed; she grew old and died before reaching her goal.

But she soon reincarnated, remembering herself as Amba and recalling Amba's intense hostility toward Bhishma. As soon as her childhood was over she again dedicated her life to intense austerity and prayer. Her mind was so focused on her goal that her own welfare was meaningless to her. She sat in meditation for such a long time that she lost body-consciousness. Finally, in a state of deep meditation, she received a boon in the field of her intuition: she knew that in the next lifetime she would accomplish her goal. Soon after, that life too came to an end.

Next she reincarnated as Prince Shikhandi, the son of King Drupada. Once again her memory was intact—the prince remembered himself as Amba, the princess of Banaras, and this memory was so clear that he formed a strong identification with her. In his interior life, his father's empire and all royal pleasures held no value to him, but he used his princely privileges to master the science of archery, and by and by he grew to be a great warrior. Although he was still no match for Bhishma, the prince remembered that he had been granted the boon of killing him in this lifetime. He did not know how he would do it, but full of faith, he waited for the right circumstance to present itself.

Bhishma was still a vibrant warrior, unmatched by anyone on earth even though by now he was 180 years old. At this time the grandchildren of his stepbrothers were waging a war against each other and Bhishma had no choice but to join the battle as commander-in-chief of one side. Shikhandi joined the forces that stood against Bhishma.

Before the war began Bhishma had established rules, which both parties had agreed to follow, and one of them was that a man must not raise a weapon against a woman. He set this rule even though he knew intuitively that Prince Shikhandi was Amba, the princess of Banaras, who, intent on avenging herself on him, had been incarnating one life after another in order to do so. Finally, after nine bloody days of battle, Bhishma was confronted with Shikhandi, and obeying the rules he himself had established, he dropped his weapons rather than raise them against the princess Amba. Shikhandi and his ally, Arjuna, showered Bhishma with arrows, badly wounding him. He fell to the ground, never to get up again. Thus Prince Shikhandi accomplished the goal of his life.

Some souls, because of their strong will, their practice of austerities and prayer, and their power of determination, reincarnate to complete the work they were intent on accomplishing in their previous life. From a spiritual perspective, Amba's three lifetimes were a complete waste. Instead of using her indomitable power of will for a higher purpose, she squandered it on vengeance. And by doing so, God alone knows what negative karma she incurred.

Even an incarnated soul must understand the value of life

and use clarity of mind and the power of determination in order to continue advancing on the path of spiritual unfoldment. As the mythologies of many of the world's religions tell us, demons and destructive souls have the power to reincarnate just as spiritually evolved souls do. But this ability neither transforms them into divine beings nor enables them to unveil the mystery of death and birth and the truth that lies beyond. What does enable a soul to become immortal is sadhana nourished by grace.

It is through sadhana that we advance on the path of inner unfoldment until we reach a state where no samskaras remain in our inner realm. That state, as previously mentioned, is known as *nirbija* (seedless) samadhi. The emergence of that state is preceded by a state of spiritual development known as *dharma megha* samadhi (*Yoga Sutra* 4:29–32). *Dharma megha* means "cloud of virtues," and refers to spiritual samskaras that are unalloyed by other samskaras. Figuratively speaking, in this state our virtuous samskaras are like clouds that continually extinguish the fire of negative karmas and samskaras. Then, when all the negative samskaras are totally extinguished, the powerful wind of *vairagya*—the highest form of dispassion—arises and sweeps away even the cloud of virtues. This powerful wind is generated by divine grace, which wishes us to be free even of our good deeds. And when all our karmas and samskaras disappear, there arises the highest state of spiritual absorption, *nirbija* samadhi. We are confronted with obstacles only until we reach *dharma megha* samadhi, for beyond this point there are no karmas or samskaras to create obstacles.

Once they have gained access to seedless samadhi, yogis have perfect freedom to leave their bodies at will. After reaching this state of realization, they can be active in the world and yet remain unaffected by their actions because their actions are no longer motivated by self-interest. As long as they maintain their bodies it is irrelevant what lifestyle they adopt because internally they are always established in the essential self.

The kings Janaka and Ikshvaku were yogis of this caliber; so were the merchant Tuladhara, the butcher Dharmavyadha, the weaver Kabir, and the cobbler Raidas. These reincarnated souls dedicated their lives to spiritual practice and attained such a high level of realization that the world and so-called worldly actions had no power to affect their inner awareness. Due to the light of inner knowledge their power of nonattachment was so great that they could experientially disidentify themselves from their minds—and thus from the subtle impressions deposited there—as well as from their bodies.

For them, casting off the body and returning its elements to nature was as easy as removing our clothes and sending them to the laundry is for us. And the ability to voluntarily cast off the body gives these adepts freedom to return to this world voluntarily. Their death is not an ordinary death, but rather a departure from the body, and if they return, this return cannot be categorized as birth. As previously stated, the scriptures call such a re-embodiment *divya janma,* divine birth, or divine emergence.

The essence of spirituality lies in unveiling the mystery of divine birth, for as Lord Krishna says in the Bhagavad Gita (4:9), "One who precisely knows that both my births and actions are of divine origin, after casting off the body that person does not fall into the grip of rebirth, but instead reaches me."

CHAPTER EIGHT

DIVINE BIRTH:
THE WAY OF THE SAGES

THE MYSTERY OF DIVINE BIRTH can be unraveled only by the immortal sages who have experienced the immortal self and can distinguish it from the mortal self (composed of the body, the breath, and the conscious and unconscious mind). This knowledge has enabled them to discover the method for consciously and deliberately casting off the physical body, and so the privilege of returning to this world through divine birth is theirs alone.

Casting Off the Body

There are many techniques for casting off the body voluntarily, some of which are still practiced by Himalayan adepts. Sri Swami Rama describes three of these in his book *Living with the Himalayan Masters*: *hima* samadhi, *jala* samadhi, and *sthala* samadhi. Hima samadhi involves casting off the body in deep snow. This is done by sitting in meditation under the open sky, entering a deep state of samadhi, and allowing the body to freeze. When this technique is done under water it is called jala samadhi; underground, it is called sthala samadhi.

These and other yogic methods of casting off the body voluntarily are not to be confused with the act of suicide, for unlike suicides, yogis are free from mental and psychological turmoil. They drop the body not in response to an emotional upheaval, but when they realize the purpose of having a body has been accomplished. They neither lust for life nor have an aversion to it. For them, the act of willfully giving the elements of the body back to nature is like the act of returning apartment keys to the landlord when the lease has expired.

Hima, jala, and sthala samadhi are by no means the only methods yogic adepts use for casting off the body. Another technique, also touched on in *Living with the Himalayan Masters,* entails leaving through the navel center. This method is possible only for those who have cultivated *yoga agni* (yogic fire) through intense and prolonged practice. The body of such a yogi is transformed or purified by yogic fire and is therefore free from disease. When it is time to drop the body, these yogis ignite the inner flame at the solar plexus with such intensity that the body is instantly consumed by fire, and by so doing they become one with the sun. As everything in our world is illuminated and sustained by the light of the sun, our world is also pervaded by the consciousness of these adepts. They are pure light, but they can appear and disappear at will by assuming a physical body. They usually return to this world only through divine birth.

———

Sometimes, for the good of humanity, yoga masters take on a prolonged and painful ordeal—disease or other injury—

before casting off the body. For example, the *Mahabharata* describes how the great yogi Bhishma left his body in a most extraordinary way. As we saw in the previous chapter, he dropped his weapons and stopped fighting at the sight of Prince Shikhandi, who, according to Bhishma's high standards, was still Princess Amba. When Bhishma allowed himself to become totally defenseless, Shikhandi and Arjuna showered him with arrows with such force that many of them drove all the way through his body and protruded from the other side. He fell and lay suspended by them, but chose not to leave his body for another six months because he had vowed to remain embodied until the kingdom was secure.

After the war was over, and the corpses had been removed from the battlefield, an assembly of sages and kings gathered around the still-living Bhishma. From sunrise to sunset he lay on his bed of arrows greeting the sages and imparting knowledge to the kings and other spiritual seekers, and refused to allow thirst, tiredness, and pain to come close to him. At the end of the day, however, he invited discomfort, as well as sickness, disease, old age, and the fruits of his known and unknown karmas (which he had been disregarding his whole life) to claim their rights on his body. Thus he allowed suffering to claim him only at night.

When six months had passed, and with the permission of the sages and Lord Krishna, he gathered his pranic forces. With the help of breath retention *(kumbhaka)* he packed his body with prana from toe to head so tightly that all the arrows popped out, and in a few seconds his body, which had been so full of holes that it resembled a sieve, was healed. After offering his homage to Lord Krishna and the assembled sages, Bhishma cast off his body.

Returning to the World of Death and Birth

According to yogic scriptures the most sublime way to cast off the body is through the *sahasrara,* the thousand-petaled lotus at the crown center, which is reached through the *brahma nadi* or *brahma loka.* Only perfect masters gain access to this *nadi;* those who have gained direct experience of this realm make mystical statements such as "I and my Father are one," "I am Brahman," "I am the way, the truth, and the life." Yogis leaving their bodies through the crown chakra can come into this world in any fashion they choose. Totally free, they are one with the Divine. The sole reason for their return is compassion—the active will of the Divine. It motivates these souls to walk in the flesh and help those struggling in the realm of death and rebirth. Their way of returning to this world is always shrouded in mystery, which is why there are extraordinary stories relating to the birth of such great ones as Rama, Krishna, Buddha, and Christ.

According to the spiritual history of India, Rama's father, King Dhasharatha, and his three wives had almost lost hope of having children. In desperation they consulted their guru, sage Vasishtha, who advised them to undertake a special spiritual practice known as *putreshti yajna.* At the conclusion of this practice, a bowl filled with rice pudding emerged from the ceremonial fire and a voice came from the sky advising Dhasharatha to distribute the pudding to his wives, who would be blessed with children. Soon after, Rama and his three brothers were born.

Although all four children emerged in an extraordinary way, the emergence of the eldest, Rama, was particularly striking. Rama's mother had no labor pains but entered a trance-like state in which she saw a radiant baby with four arms. Overwhelmed by the vision, she prayed to the child: "Withdraw your brilliance, O Lord, for it is unbearable to my senses. Please assume the form of a baby so that I can love and serve you as your mother." The radiant four-armed baby instantly turned into a normal infant and began to cry.

Krishna's birth was similar. His mother, Deviki, and her husband, Vasudeva, were in prison at the time. Deviki had all the signs of pregnancy, but did not go into labor. She simply woke from a deep sleep to find the baby Krishna lying next to her, and all signs of pregnancy gone. It was as if a spell had been cast on everyone in the immediate vicinity—the guards fell asleep, the prison doors opened as if by themselves. Because the king who had imprisoned the couple had vowed to kill any male baby of Deviki's, Vasudeva carried the baby to a village across the Yamuna River in the midst of a dark and rainy night. There he entered the house of a close friend, placed baby Krishna next to his friend's sleeping wife, and carried her newborn daughter back to prison with him. The moment he reentered his prison cell, both he and his wife forgot everything that had transpired. Later they regained their memories, and thus Krishna was claimed by two sets of parents.

Buddha's mother gave birth to him while standing in a forest; moments afterward, the infant walked seven steps. Christ was born of a virgin mother, in what is called an immaculate birth.

———

The births of Rama, Krishna, Buddha, and Christ, while shrouded in mystery, are at least associated with human parents in some way, which makes them somewhat comprehensible to us. But many of these masters return through a nonhuman medium. Their stories can lead us to a deeper understanding of divine birth.

According to the yoga tradition, the eternal sage Narayana himself walks in the flesh in the form of the great master Matsyendra Natha. Approximately 1,500 years ago, realizing the depth of human ignorance and misery, he resolved to help the human race through a beloved disciple who had already left his body and become one with universal consciousness.

One day as Matsyendra Natha traveled through a village in search of parents for his immortal son, he stopped at a house for alms. When the housewife offered him flour, the yogi explained that he had no place to prepare it, so the woman willingly made a fire and helped him cook his meal. When the yogi had eaten, rested, and was preparing to depart, the woman came to say goodbye. Pleased with her hospitality, Matsyendra Natha asked if she wished a special blessing from him. She replied sadly that she was barren and everyone, even members of her own family, avoided her because they considered her to be inauspicious. Filled with compassion, the yogi picked up some ash from the fire pit and handed it to her, saying "Eat a pinch of this ash and rub the rest on your body. You will definitely have a son. He will be a great yogi and will do the work of God." With these words, Matsyendra Natha departed.

Unable to contain her excitement, the woman rushed out of the house to tell the other women in her neighborhood about the blessing of the yogi. The women ridiculed her and made fun of her barrenness. One woman remarked, "Ash! What a remarkable cure for barrenness. Hah! Make peace with your misfortune and live like trash." Another woman, who was a little kinder, said, "Just to get their food, these wandering yogis say such things. It's all right that you gave him food, but don't be fooled by him." The barren woman now thought that if her husband and in-laws heard that she had been rubbing ash all over her body they would think she was crazy as well as inauspicious. So, wishing to avoid further trouble, she decided not to do as Matsyendra Natha had advised; instead she gathered up all the ash and threw it in the family compost pit.

Twelve years passed, and Matsyendra Natha decided to pay a visit to the child who was his eternal son and student. Once again he traveled to the village and stopped at the house of the woman he had blessed. To his surprise, she told him that she had no child. "I gave you a child!" he said adamantly. "How is it possible that he is not with you? What happened to the ash?" Upon hearing that she had thrown it in the compost pit, he demanded that she take him there. When she did, Matsyendra Natha gazed at the pit and called, *"Alakh Niranjan"* (this literally means "One who can neither be seen nor tainted"). Immediately a radiant twelve-year-old adolescent emerged from the pit. He bowed to his master, and the two walked away. This young man later came to be known as Guru Gorakha Natha.

As this story illustrates, the sages of Guru Gorakha Natha's caliber are literally the word of God in flesh. At the behest of his master, this immortal yogi has been guiding sincere aspirants for more than a millennium. Even today we hear occasional reports from those who have met and received guidance from him.

Divine Sport

Just as we entertain ourselves through worldly sports, the immortal sages entertain themselves through divine sport, *lila*. Their game begins with divine birth and ends when they withdraw from the mortal frame. It is inspired by the divine will and so it has a purpose ordinarily incomprehensible to our limited minds. But in one way or another the actions of such sages—even their very presence—dispel the darkness of ignorance which binds us to this mortal plane. The divine birth of Shuka Deva provides a glimpse of the immortal sages at play in the subtle realm, occupied with games which can be seen and understood only by those blessed with *divya chakshu* (divine eyes). With our limited knowledge we cannot always comprehend why an immortal sage comes to this world. But the scriptures tell us that both their birth and the actions they perform during their lifetime are of divine origin. In the context of the divine birth of Shuka Deva, we may surmise that the purpose of his birth was to bring forth the *Srimad Bhagavatam*, one of the foremost scriptures of *bhakti* yoga. The story of this divine birth unfolds in the following manner.

Sage Narada is known for his mysterious and often seemingly mischievous games. Intent on doing something for the benefit of humanity, one morning he visited Shiva's ashram on Mount Kailash. Upon arriving, he found that Shiva had gone to Badrinath to see Narayana. Narada was delighted: he'd been hoping to find that Shiva was not at home. Assuming a sad face he greeted Shiva's wife, Parvati, who asked him what was the matter.

"Nothing, Mother," he replied. "I'm all right. Where is Shiva? I don't see him here."

"He is visiting Narayana and will be back in the afternoon. But please tell me, why do you look so sad today? Is there anything I can do?"

"Leave me with my sorrow, Mother," Narada replied. Then, with a deep sigh, he continued, "Wherever I go I see the same drama and hear the same story. It looks like maya has spread its wings everywhere in the universe. Now I think I should move on."

This made Parvati even more curious: "No, no, Narada. You must tell me what's making you sad. I will not let you go until you do."

"Don't press me, Mother, because you will not be happy to hear it nor will I be happy to tell you. If you really want to relieve my sorrow, then tell me a place where I can go and forget this world."

"But you must tell me, Narada," she insisted.

"There is so much cheating and deception everywhere," Narada said. "Even so, I thought that at least your household would be free from duplicity. I am so disappointed."

"Cheating and deception in my household? I don't believe you, Narada."

"That's why I was hesitating to tell you, Mother," Narada said gently. "You are innocent and you will not understand it."

"What will I not understand?"

"Shiva is cheating you—that is what you will not understand. I don't say he loves someone else, but I can certainly tell you that he does not love you as much as he says he does. The thing he loves the most he hides from you."

"What is it that he hides from me, Narada?" Parvati asked.

"Before I answer your question, Mother, let me first ask you something. Whose skulls does Shiva wear as a garland?"

"They are my skulls," Parvati replied. "He loves me so much that he preserves the skull every time I leave my body, and wears it as a remembrance of me."

"That means you have been constantly dying and being born, while he himself remains the same. Why? Because he knows the immortal tale, the *Srimad Bhagavatam,* and because of this he has become immortal. He knows that whoever hears that tale becomes immortal, but he has never told it to you because he does not want this to happen to you.

"What is this so-called love that lets you die only to be reborn? This business of wearing your skulls does not make sense to me. He could have shared the immortal knowledge and you could also have become immortal, living with him happily forever. You may think he loves you selflessly and unconditionally, but I don't. All these experiences make me grateful that I am not married.

"Let me go now, Mother. If Shiva comes back and finds you sad he will hold me responsible." So saying, Narada left.

Parvati pretended not to be affected, but deep down she was so perturbed that she even forgot to ask Narada to have lunch before he left.

Shortly afterwards Shiva returned and found the ashram unusually quiet. Right away he went into Parvati's chamber, but Parvati pretended not to notice him. She did not even respond when Shiva greeted her. Puzzled, he finally asked, "Are you not feeling well, Parvati?"

"Why do you need to know such things?" she countered. "Go and enjoy your samadhi or have fun with your friends and devotees." With these words, she walked out.

Shiva asked Ganesha, Skanda, Nandi, and other members of the family what had happened, but nobody could tell him why Parvati was upset. At dinner time there was nothing to eat. When the children asked for food, Parvati said, "Go and ask your father." Thus they were hungry all night.

In the morning Shiva, using all his charm and wisdom, tried to find the cause of his wife's displeasure, but to no avail. After many unsuccessful attempts, he finally asked, "Was Narada here yesterday?"

"Yes, he was here, but why should you care?" Parvati retorted.

Shiva laughed. "Then it is Narada who put our home on fire. Tell me, what did he say?"

After some cajoling Parvati told him. Then she asked, "Why is it that you have never told me that immortal tale?"

Shiva replied, "Since you never asked, I did not tell you. Today you are asking, and I will certainly tell you, but only on the condition that no one else be present. By hearing this tale one becomes immortal, so I want only deserving people to listen to it. Anyone who hears it without my permission will be slain by me. Let us go into solitude so that no one other than you will hear me tell it."

All this time Narada was intuitively keeping track of the interaction between Shiva and his wife. When he realized that Shiva would not allow anyone to be present while he recited the immortal tale to Parvati, he was downcast for a moment. But another plan flashed into his mind. He went to sage Shuka Deva and told him about this special event, and asked Shuka Deva to be there to hear Shiva recite the scripture.

Shuka Deva knew that there must be something fishy about this request, so he asked, "How come you are allowing your ears to be deprived of this elixir?"

"Shiva will slay whoever hears this tale without his permission," Narada explained. "He has agreed to recite it only to Parvati; that is the reason I want you to go and listen quietly."

"What great advice!" said Shuka Deva. "What are you going to gain from my being slain?"

"I promise to protect you," said Narada. "Please go. Hide yourself somewhere. Listen to the tale and use your retentive power to memorize it. Later on, make the wisdom available to the spiritual seekers on earth."

With this, Shuka Deva agreed. He checked out the surroundings in his subtle body and noticed an unfertilized parrot's egg under the boulder where Shiva and Parvati planned to sit for the recitation. Using his yogic power, he entered the egg.

Shiva began to recite. Brimming with the joy of the recitation, he closed his eyes. From time to time Parvati expressed her delight, saying "Umm, wonderful," "Hmm, marvelous." But as the long recitation neared its end, Parvati began to doze and stopped murmuring.

By this time the egg had hatched, and Shuka Deva was under the boulder in the parrot chick's body. He was afraid that since Parvati had stopped saying "Hmm" Shiva might open his eyes and, finding her asleep, stop the recitation. So Shuka Deva the parrot began to say "Hmm" in place of Parvati—and Shiva kept his eyes closed until he had completed the recitation. Then he opened his eyes and asked Parvati if she had heard all twelve sections of the tale.

Startled, Parvati opened her eyes and said, "No, Lord. I heard only ten. I think I must have fallen asleep."

"Then who was saying 'Hmm' while you were asleep?"

Shiva roared. "There must be someone hiding here."

With his trident in hand, he leapt up to find the intruder. Terrified, Shuka Deva took flight as fast as he could. Shiva unleashed his trident in the direction of the young parrot. Seeing this, Narada fled instantly to Narayana and cried, "Help! Help, O Lord! Shuka Deva is in trouble. There's no time to explain. Shiva is furious with Shuka Deva and you are the only one who can prevent him from being destroyed by Shiva's trident."

Narayana replied, "But Narada, Shiva's trident is the unfailing weapon of the universe. I have no reason to violate the laws which have been established by nature. How can I interfere? The only way to help Shuka Deva would be for a Brahma rishi [a sage of the highest level of self-realization] to stand between him and Shiva's trident. The problem is that just as I cannot interfere without a justifiable reason, neither can a Brahma rishi."

"But," Narayana continued, "if Shuka Deva were to be born as Vyasa's son, then it would become Vyasa's duty to protect him. It is up to you, Narada, to figure out how Vyasa can have a son even though he has no wife."

Instantly a plan flashed into Narada's mind. With poor Shuka Deva still flying desperately across the sky hotly pursued by Shiva's trident, Narada asked an adept yogini, Ghritachi, to appear in front of Vyasa in her most enticing form precisely at the moment he opened his eyes to offer an oblation into the holy fire.

"The moment Vyasa looks at Ghritachi," Narada then told Shuka Deva, "the thought will spontaneously flash into his mind that she is a beautiful woman. At this moment, drop your bird's body and jump into Ghritachi's womb.

Then call your father Vyasa for help."

The plan went off perfectly. At exactly the right moment Shuka Deva entered Ghritachi's womb and cried, "Father, help, help! I'm scared of Shiva's trident!"

Realizing that it is a father's duty to serve and protect his son in every situation, Vyasa stood between the trident and Ghritachi, with the entire power and brilliance of his *tapas* (ascetic practice). Narayana and Narada then went to Shiva and asked, "How can you slay someone who, by your own decree, has become immortal by hearing the immortal tale from you?"

Shiva laughed. "I love your mischief, Narada," he said, and withdrew his trident.

After remaining in his mother's womb for twelve years, Shuka Deva emerged as an infant, but instantly grew into a twelve-year-old boy, his mind so absorbed in Krishna that the scriptures say he looked like another Krishna. The present version of the *Srimad Bhagavatam,* which he recited under the banyan tree at Shukatal in northern India, is Shuka Deva's gift to humankind. This version also documents the advanced yogic practices Shuka Deva undertook, and these are a source of inspiration to sincere seekers.

All the sages involved in the process of Shuka Deva's divine birth are immortal. We who are mortal have no context for understanding why Narada set about giving mortals the gift of the *Srimad Bhagavatam* in such a convoluted, mischievous fashion, nor can we grasp Shuka Deva's way of dropping his natural body, entering the egg of the parrot, emerging from it in the chick's body, and then entering the womb of Ghritachi. To learned seekers divine birth is shrouded in mystery, while to the ignorant it is totally confusing and seemingly impossible. Thus some of us consider these stories to be literally true and others take them as myth.

Experimenting with Death

After attaining victory over the forces that govern the process of destruction, death, and decay, the immortal masters played with death in order to unveil the mystery that rules nature's finer forces. They experimented fearlessly with numerous techniques for rejuvenating the body, increasing longevity, and even outrunning death. They allowed themselves to go through the process of death and birth so they could relate to the pain and pleasure centered around this process in the lives of ordinary people. In other words, although fully enlightened, they allowed ignorance to veil their consciousness for a time so that they could experience how unliberated souls feel, think, and act, in order to teach them more effectively. One notable example of this was the great sage Vasishtha, who voluntarily undertook the journey of death and rebirth to gain a clear and objective experience of this whole process.

According to the scriptures Vasishtha emerged from the mind of Brahma, and thus he had a father but no mother; or, looking at it another way, Brahma was both father and mother. Vasishtha was so spiritually evolved that the goddess of wisdom, Sarasvati, treated him as her brother, and at the behest of Brahma he undertook the job of teaching and guiding others on the path of spirituality. To make sure that his teachings would be practical to those caught in the cycle of birth and death, Vasishtha decided to cast off his body and go through at least two cycles himself, thus gaining firsthand knowledge of the turmoil and commotion involved.

Vasishtha and his wife, Arundhati, chalked out a plan: they would fall into the cycle of birth and death, but the goddess Sarasvati would help them out should they get caught. The sage Valmiki, who was endowed with infinite intuitive wisdom, documented their adventures in the scripture called the *Yoga Vasishtha*. The story goes as follows.

———

Long ago there lived a powerful and noble king named Padma. His wife, Queen Lila, was beautiful, wise, loving, and wholly dedicated to her husband. She did not want to be separated from him under any circumstance. Even though she knew that anyone born into this world must die one day, in her heart she wished that her husband could be an exception. Or, not wanting to live without him, she wished that she would die first. But as soon as she had this thought, she realized that her death would cause her husband great distress, so her greatest desire was that King Padma would live forever.

With these thoughts in mind she assembled all the wise and learned people in her kingdom, and asked if there was some way to prevent death. Although the wise people unanimously replied there was not, Queen Lila was determined to find a way.

She undertook an intense practice of meditation on the goddess Sarasvati. Because she had already been on the path of meditation and had strong devotional ties to Sarasvati, she was blessed with the vision of the goddess soon after undertaking this practice. When the goddess gave her permission to ask for a boon, Lila said that if her husband should die before she did, she would like his *jiva* (soul) to remain near her. Sarasvati granted this boon, adding that King Padma would also

materialize in his previous form whenever Lila wished. Then
the goddess disappeared.

Time passed. The couple grew old, and one day King
Padma died. Queen Lila, overcome with grief, began sobbing.
From the sky, Sarasvati's consoling voice reminded her that
the king's soul was still near, but that she should preserve King
Padma's body carefully until his life-force (prana) returned
and he was restored to life. Queen Lila was struck with delight
and wonder. With a composed mind she asked everyone to
leave the chamber, and when they were gone she meditated on
the goddess Sarasvati—who, upholding her promise, appeared
to her. After greeting her respectfully, Lila asked, "Mother,
where is my husband?"

The goddess replied, "He is in this very room, but in a different realm of creation, one that is more subtle than the realm
in which you are."

Sarasvati explained that there is a universe inside the
universe which is visible to the naked eye, and inside that
universe there is yet another. "There are an infinite number of
universes within the universe," she went on. "A universe
belonging to a particular realm of creation is totally invisible to
those living in another realm. You perceive only the universe
you are born in and only if you are equipped with the senses to
perceive it. But by harnessing the power of mind, you can transcend this natural limitation and gain access to universes existing in other realms. Harnessing such powers of mind is known
as gaining *siddhis*." Sarasvati added that Lila had all the prerequisites for attaining them.

Lila was curious to see what her husband was doing in
another, more subtle realm of existence, so Sarasvati taught her
the technique for entering other realms. And because she was

already an accomplished yogini, Lila soon became proficient. Both the queen and the goddess entered the realm where King Padma now dwelt. He was sixteen years old, and had already been crowned king. His queen was just like Lila herself had been when she was sixteen.

Turning to the goddess, Lila said, "He died just moments ago; how can he already be sixteen years old? Further, how can an entire realm and the kingdom existing therein fit into this small room?"

The goddess explained that time and space are both relative and are measured differently in different realms of existence. For example, a minute in one realm can be equivalent to several hundred years in another; conversely, an event that requires an eon in one universe may take only a moment in another. During a dream that lasts ten minutes, you may gain experience of objects and events which normally take several years in the waking state.

"In what to you seems to be a couple of minutes, your husband has been reborn and completed sixteen years of life," the goddess told Lila. "He rules a vast kingdom which fits within the space of the room in which he died. Even more surprising, in yet another realm where you and your husband were a brahmin couple before becoming King Padma and Queen Lila, a week has not yet passed since you both died. As time is measured in that realm, in that one week you and your husband have been born, you have reigned as king and queen for many years, and your husband has died of old age. And here in this realm where we are now observing him, your husband has already completed sixteen years of life. To show you the truth of what I am saying, let me take you to the universe where the cottage of this brahmin couple lies empty."

And so with the help of Sarasvati, Lila entered that realm. There she saw the empty cottage where the brahmin couple— Vasishtha and his wife, Arundhati—had lived. Sarasvati explained: "A week ago you lived in this cottage. Both of you were fully established in the wisdom of immortality. Then one day you both decided you wanted to gain firsthand experience of the cycle of death and birth so that you could teach those caught in this cycle what they need to learn. While you were discussing this plan, a royal procession passed by. You talked about how wonderful it must feel to be a king and queen and enjoy the luxuries of life. This fleeting thought turned into a strong desire, which awakened *vasanas* [subtle impressions of the past] that had accumulated in your previous lives. As these vasanas arose you lost interest in living as the sages Vasishtha and Arundhati. And with that strong vasana you left your bodies to be born as King Padma and Queen Lila.

"As a royal couple you enjoyed sensual pleasures, ruled your subjects, assigned punishments, and gave generous charitable donations. As time passed, you grew old and your husband's body was no longer a means to fulfill the purpose that he had in mind—to enjoy life as a king.

"Now let me take you to the realm where your husband is reigning as King Viduratha, whom you saw a few moments ago as a sixteen-year-old." The next moment the goddess and Lila were back with King Viduratha. Lila could not believe her eyes—both the king and his wife were now seventy years old.

Lila and Sarasvati waited until the king was alone and then made themselves visible and reminded him of his previous identity as King Padma. The memory caused the king a great deal of confusion. He was not able to disidentify from himself as King Viduratha, but at the same time he tried to remember himself as King Padma. He loved his present wife and children very much, but in his unconscious mind he was also missing the wife and children of his previous life. He was on the brink of a nervous breakdown, and while he was caught in the utter confusion engendered by attachments to two sets of families, kingdoms, and their corresponding responsibilities, his present kingdom was attacked and he suffered a mortal injury. As he was dying he began to lose the memories of his immediate past, and at some point he lost his awareness of being King Viduratha. At the moment of final departure he remembered his previous life, and that pulled forward the memories of his wife Lila and the room where he had died. This train of thought then served as a vehicle for entering that room, where his own corpse was lying preserved. The power of attachment helped him recognize the body and enabled him to enter it.

Now King Padma awoke as from a coma. Instantly he remembered his entire life as King Padma, forgetting his rebirth as King Viduratha. Standing before him were his wife and the goddess. Sarasvati's presence was a surprise to him, and as a gesture of reverence he bowed his head to her. He asked what had transpired while he slept, and Sarasvati related the entire episode of his death and rebirth, reminding him of his true identity as the sage Vasishtha. Both Lila and Padma were glad to recapture the knowledge of their previous life, as well as the mystery that surrounds the cycle of death and birth, but they wondered at their amnesia.

Sarasvati explained, "As King Padma and Queen Lila you had forgotten who you are, but as the sages Vasishtha and Arundhati neither of you had forgotten. When you were Vasishtha and Arundhati, you made a *sankalpa* [willful determination] to gain firsthand experience of birth and death and the experience of pain and pleasure that goes with it. And with this intention you deliberately created the desire to enjoy the best of the pleasures of the world for a while. As part of this sankalpa, you asked me to come and remind you of your identity as Vasishtha and Arundhati if you got caught in the cycle."

After King Padma and Queen Lila had regained their knowledge, the goddess disappeared. The couple lived afterwards as *jivan muktas* (liberated souls), handing over the kingdom to their worthy son and retiring to the forest. There in solitude they left their bodies and reidentified with the consciousness of Vasishtha and Arundhati. Thereafter this immortal couple each created a mind through the sheer power of their *asmita* (pure I-am-ness). (In yoga this self-created mind is known as *nirmana chitta* [*Yoga Sutra* 4:4–7].) And from these self-created minds each created a body identical to those they had inhabited as Vasishtha and Arundhati. Thus they were able to guide those on the spiritual path.

Preparing for Divine Birth

From his experience of the cycle of birth and death Vasishtha saw that it was the power of will and determination—*sankalpa shakti*—that pushes us on the path to either liberation or bondage. It became clear to him that as humans we have the capacity to become whatever we are determined to become, but that success in both mundane and spiritual endeavors requires an indomitable will, one in which there is no room for even the slightest doubt. An enlightened one is possessed of an unrestricted power of will and determination, and because of this the subtle impressions of the past lose their effect. But the sankalpa shakti of unenlightened souls is so weak and fragmented that the accumulated impressions of the past take over and maneuver the unconscious mind after death. Sages like Vasishtha and Arundhati use their power of sankalpa to shape their own destinies as they wish, while the multifold weak and fragmented streams of sankalpa shakti of most people collide and neutralize each other.

The world is a creation of the mind—it emerges from, and is reabsorbed into, the mind of its creator. Within the larger world we all inhabit, each of us creates our own little world. With the threads of imagination we weave notions of success, failure, loss, gain, pleasure, pain, and a host of other ideas and feelings. When we die our world unravels, but we carry the subtle impressions of it with us, and using those subtle impressions as building materials we create our world again; thus we are reborn.

It is only after a long practice of purification and meditation, accompanied by *vairagya* (nonattachment) and divine grace, that we can begin to extricate ourselves from the cycle of death and rebirth. When we have created strong spiritual samskaras through these means we are able to die with relative awareness, and this makes it possible to reincarnate. From this point on we have the opportunity to make speedy progress in our spiritual journey.

Each of us comes into a body with a different degree of awareness and freedom, and we have no way of knowing if we have been reborn or reincarnated. Reincarnated souls do not usually know who they were in their past lives, what kind of practices they did during that life, or what particular karma brought them to this world. Their life circumstances are led by the force of destiny, which remains a mystery to them. Nature or destiny arranges circumstances so that they are able to pick up their practices where they left off in their previous life, but even so they must face a host of obstacles, including sickness and old age. They must be vigilant regarding their practice and must make sure that it is intense enough to burn their samskaras before life comes to an end. If not, they have to reincarnate again.

Even though we do not know if we have been reborn or reincarnated, either way we must strive to accomplish the purpose of human life, for, as the *Ramayana* says, once we lose this opportunity it is difficult to get another. We must not postpone accomplishing our goal until the next lifetime. Guru Gorakha Natha emphatically states: "Shame on the aspirant who claims to be sincere but dies without accomplishing the purpose of life. And shame on the teacher who claims to be a *sad guru* [adept master] if his disciple dies before reaching the goal."

From this we can see that the guru/disciple relationship is not to be taken lightly. Fully realized masters may have many followers and devotees, but they rarely accept disciples. And once they do accept a disciple, they are committed to lead their disciple all the way to the attainment of immortality.

To make sure that their disciples do not go through unnecessary reincarnations, the masters teach them systematic methods of knowing themselves at every level—body, breath, mind, and soul. Common to all yogic practices are basic principles for maintaining a healthy body, developing a one-pointed mind, and living in the world while yet remaining unaffected by it. Once an aspirant is fully established in these basic practices, the master imparts specific techniques which enable them to unveil the deeper mysteries of life for themselves. The advanced practices of hatha yoga, kundalini yoga, nada yoga, mantra yoga, or tantra yoga are among them. The scriptures tell us that the masters may introduce rejuvenation techniques and methods for increasing longevity to those who are so determined to break all their inner knots that they have fully dedicated their lives to the practice. This is done to enable the disciple to undertake an intense practice for a prolonged period of time without interruption and thus reach the goal in this lifetime.

The scriptures also tell us of a technique called *parakaya pravesha* which adept yogis occasionally employ either to continue their own practice without interruption or to guide their disciples without interruption. *Parakaya pravesha* is a technique for casting off one's body and entering another, but the spiritual laws that govern entering a fully mature body are quite clear. Yogis may use their yogic ability to cast off an old body and enter a new one only at the will of the Divine this process cannot be engendered in response to a personal wish. In addition, a yogi may enter another body only after the original occupant has left it. In other words, the yogi must enter a corpse and bring it back to life solely through the yogi's powers. Under these circumstances the body will have gone through some degree of decomposition, and some of the organs may have lost their capacity to function. Therefore in order to apply this technique a yogi must have both the knowledge and the capacity to revive, rejuvenate, and detoxify the body so that it becomes habitable. Fully realized masters impart this knowledge only to fully prepared disciples, and if this *kriya* (literally, "performance") is beyond the capacity of the disciple, the master will find the disciple again after the disciple has reincarnated. It is in this context that the scriptures say, "When the disciple is prepared, the master appears."

There are also highly esoteric practices, such as meditation on one of the *mahavidyas* (literally, "great sciences") known as *chhinnmasta,* that can be completed only by undergoing physical death. Once they have undertaken this practice, advanced yogis may fulfill this requirement through *parakaya pravesha*—they cast off the body in which the practice was undertaken and enter another to complete the practice.

In order to attain the mastery that makes such practices possible, each of us must identify our own place on the path and start from there. We will never free ourselves from the grip of maya if we allow ourselves to believe we are advanced, incarnated souls and thus need only advanced practices. If even great souls can fall into the snares of maya, as documented in the *Ramayana* and other scriptures, then certainly anyone can fall into its trap. To reach the summit of self-realization we must commit ourselves to a systematic practice which enables us to purify our mind and heart, loosen the knots of our karmas, neutralize the effects of negative samskaras, and strengthen our willpower and determination. A practice can never be effective unless it is accompanied by *vairagya* (non–attachment) and the grace of God. All the components fall into place when we come into the company of spiritually inspired people *(satsanga)* who prescribe practices suited to each individual. So let us explore where and how to begin the journey toward immortality.

CHAPTER NINE

PRACTICES LEADING TO
HEAVEN AND BEYOND

THE SAGES HAVE DIVIDED the vast range of spiritual practices into three main categories. One set of practices helps us live a happy and healthy life while in this world. Another set ensures a graceful departure, the acquisition of heavenly delights, and return to this world to complete our spiritual journey. The third and highest set consists of techniques that enable us to transcend earth and heaven altogether by freeing ourselves from the cycle of death and birth. The *Katha Upanishad,* which is the story of Nachiketa's journey to liberation, gives a beautiful description of the vast range of spiritual practices in these three categories.

The essence of Nachiketa's story is that achieving liberation is like climbing a mountain: the only way to reach the summit is to traverse the lower slopes and make our way to the higher. The lower slopes are in no way inferior to the higher. They are a necessary part of the journey, but they are only a stage. Attachment to the fruits of the lower stages saps our enthusiasm and motivation for climbing to the higher ones, and this is what prevents us from reaching the summit. Nachiketa's story is our own story. It goes like this:

Nachiketa was a sincere young seeker, full of enthusiasm, courage, and honesty. He practiced what he believed with perfect accuracy. His father, known throughout the land for his knowledge, riches, and generosity, had already reached the peak of worldly success—he had acquired ample wealth and achieved much honor. Now he was interested in securing a high place in heaven. Following religious injunctions he began a practice consisting of meditation, recitation of the scriptures, and making a fire offering. In its last phase, the practice required that he give away his wealth to learned and needy people.

Nachiketa was fascinated with the essence of this practice, which demanded that his father give up everything—his entire wealth, and his dearest possessions, including his ego. But as a faithful son, the young seeker noticed that his father showed signs of strong attachment to his wealth. In those days cows were like cash—and his father was giving away old, sick cows which were virtually useless, and keeping the healthy ones. He also noticed that his father was becoming irritable. Nachiketa wished the best for his father and wanted him to complete the practice in all its purity and fullness. For this inspired young man, worldly objects were of little value; compromising the great merits of the practice for the sake of that which is trivial and ephemeral made no sense to him. He wanted his father to do the practice genuinely rather than just put on a show, so Nachiketa humbly tried to encourage him to overcome his attachment and give away healthy, productive cows rather than simply unloading the old, useless ones. Nachiketa also assumed his father would give him to an enlightened spiritual teacher to guide his sadhana. Children were considered to be the property of their parents in those days, and Nachiketa knew that the practice his father was doing required him to give up his dearest possessions as well as his wealth of cows. So he went to his father and asked to whom he would be given. His father made no answer but showed signs of agitation. And when Nachiketa persisted, asking this question again and again, his father burst out angrily, "I give you to death!"

Nachiketa took this response positively. Instead of getting upset, he began to contemplate: "Look at those who were born and died before me. Look at those who will be born and die hence. For those who are ignorant, life is like a crop which is repeatedly being planted and harvested." From his pure and tender heart came a powerful voice: "Parents always want the best for their children. Today my father has handed me over to death. There must be something auspicious for me in this meeting."

His positive and composed mind helped Nachiketa realize that meeting death did not mean he must commit suicide. Rather it meant that he must seek and find one who understands the complete mystery of death so that Nachiketa could attain victory over it and become immortal. People who are afraid of death and who therefore have limited courage cannot meet such masters, regardless of how long they seek them. But Nachiketa thought of his father's emotional outburst as a blessing and set out to find such a master.

He eventually arrived at the door of Yamaraja, the king of death, a mortal who had become immortal through his sadhana. Yamaraja was not in, but Nachiketa was determined to gain knowledge from this master, so he waited patiently for three days and three nights without food or water. When Yamaraja returned and found the young man waiting outside his door, he said, "O learned brahmin, I bow to you; may God bless you. Since you have waited for me three days and three nights without eating or drinking, you may ask for three boons."

Nachiketa replied, "May my father regain his peace of mind. May he become cheerful and may he be free from anger. Upon my return from here, may he acknowledge me as his son."

Yamaraja blessed Nachiketa with the following boon: "Aruni, your father, will become the way he used to be. Free from anger and mental anguish, he will sleep well at night."

Then the master asked Nachiketa what he wanted for his second boon. Nachiketa replied, "I have heard that in heaven there is no fear or old age. People are free from hunger and thirst. But only those who have transcended worries enjoy life there. I know you know the science of fire that unveils the mystery of heaven. I ask that you teach it to me, endowed as I am with faith."

Yamaraja happily imparted this knowledge. He explained how the fire that unveils the mystery of heaven resides in the interior cave of the human being and in what respect it is the origin of the universe. He also explained how the pit that contains this fire is made. To make sure Nachiketa grasped the knowledge accurately and properly, the master asked him to repeat it to him, which Nachiketa did without error. Overjoyed with Nachiketa's accurate understanding of what he had been taught, the master gave him an additional blessing: from that time forward, this fire would be known as *Nachiketa agni.*

The master was so pleased with his disciple that he poured out another blessing. "May you receive this necklace consisting of multifarious beads," he said. Through this blessing the master was indirectly preparing Nachiketa for *ichchha siddhi,* which fulfills all wishes. As the *Katha Upanishad* states, by gathering the knowledge of Nachiketa agni, the aspirant transcends worries and mental anguish, cuts asunder the snares of death, and delights in heavenly pleasure.

After Nachiketa had received and absorbed the second boon, the master gave him permission to ask for the third. The wise disciple made the following request: "In regard to a person who has left this world, there are many hypotheses. One is that the soul continues to exist after death; another is that it does not. While studying and practicing under your discipline, may I gain this knowledge."

This brief request encompasses several interrelated questions: Who are we? Where did we come from? Is it possible to stop the cycle of death and birth once and for all? After this cycle ends do we continue to exist in some form? Is it possible to become immortal? Before and after we gain freedom from transmigration, what is our relationship with the absolute truth? What are the practical techniques for attaining knowledge of immortality and thereby becoming immortal?

In response to Nachiketa's condensed and concentrated question, the master replied, "Even people living in heaven are not clear on this question. It is extremely subtle and therefore almost impossible to communicate through words or even thoughts. Ask for anything except this. Ask for long life, several children and grandchildren, and unlimited wealth, and I will grant it. Ask for land the size of your imagination, and for yourself, ask to live as long as you want to live. Or ask for anything which you think to be equal to the boon you just asked, but please, Nachiketa, do not insist on that boon. Have all these beautiful chariots, horses, honor, fame, wealth, or anything which fits in your mind. Or I can turn you into a wish-yielding pot—so that anything you desire will manifest in your life."

Nachiketa remained unmoved by these temptations, and his resolve melted Yamaraja's heart. Nachiketa had passed the last test, and his master gladly imparted the knowledge of immortality and systematically taught his disciple the method of identifying the pranic forces and the channels through which they flow. He explained how these energy channels become entangled, forming knots which the seeker of immortality must disentangle in order to allow the energies to flow unhindered. He also explained that our desires and attachments are what bind us to the body, and that attaining freedom from them frees us from slavery to this mortal frame.

———

The sages have used Nachiketa's story as a model for the spiritual journey each of us makes. The first boon tells us that before we set our foot on the path, we must make peace within ourselves and with others. A person struggling with interpersonal relationships has no time and energy for higher pursuits. Day-to-day trivial concerns consume energy which could otherwise be used for understanding the more subtle mysteries of life. The first boon also implies that mere intellectual knowledge is not enough to improve the quality of our interpersonal relationships. Despite our good intentions and our knowledge of philosophy and psychology, many of us become victims of our attachments, desires, anger, greed, ego, and fear. We may be good at diagnosing others' problems but we fail to recognize those problems in ourselves, which is why we react abruptly and treat our loved ones badly. This creates an environment of tension and unhappiness. Lacking in introspection and caught in negative thinking patterns, we blame others and others blame us. Life turns into a catalog of complaints.

As all of us know from personal experience, these problems wreak havoc in both body and mind, disrupting the normal functions of pranic energies, which hold the body and mind together. There is a direct link between problems of this sort and energy blockage at the two lowest chakras; that is, tension in our interpersonal relationships causes disturbance in the energies of the first two chakras, which in turn causes the organs in our pelvic and abdominal region to become weak and diseased. Much of our consciousness is occupied by the issues relating to the first two chakras, which leaves little time or energy for exploring the wealth that lies in the higher chakras.

According to yogic and tantric scriptures, the first two chakras are enveloped by darkness and are only faintly illuminated by the sun and moon; even this faint illumination can be perceived only if we have eyes to see. During sleep or at the time of death, the mind that has not transcended the first two chakras and their corresponding issues falls into a dense darkness. It stumbles blindly in the dark territory of its unconscious, constantly tumbling into the vortices created by the subtle impressions of its own karmas. That is called hell. Overcoming these problems by imbibing the wisdom contained in Nachiketa's first boon is the goal of the initial stage of practice.

The First Steps

We have embarked on the first stage of the spiritual journey when we begin to cultivate a positive and composed mind. The first prerequisite for a higher spiritual understanding is an uncomplicated mind, one which knows the value of a simple and relaxed life and has formed the habit of forgiving and forgetting. If we are caught up in our thinking, busily nursing grudges and complexes, it is impossible to live peacefully. Under the sway of a chaotic mind we lose our decisive power and waste our time in random thoughts and actions. We have no way of knowing where our duty lies—and unless we learn to pay off our karmic obligations by performing our duties selflessly, lovingly, and skillfully, we will be caught in the cycle of birth and death.

Yamaraja imparted the knowledge and practices needed in the first stage of the journey in a very short time because he was a perfect master and Nachiketa a fully prepared student. Nachiketa was already free from emotional turmoil, his understanding of life was so profound that he did not consider his father to be unfair or abusive, and his mind was so clear that the question of forgiving and forgetting never arose. His heart was imbued with deep compassion—he wanted his father to be free of anger and greed.

The techniques for cultivating a clear, composed mind have been elaborated from different perspectives in a number of scriptures. They are mainly contemplative techniques—tools for introspection, self-analysis, and self-observation. They consist of certain "don'ts" and certain "dos"—restraints and observances. On the path of simplicity and purity, these principles are as indispensable as food and breath. In the yoga tradition they are known as the *yamas* and *niyamas*.

Yamas, the restraints, consist of five principles: nonviolence, nonlying, nonstealing, nonsensuality, and nonpossessiveness. Practicing them helps us become healthy and civilized members of our families and communities. They cut down on distractions and reduce the problems we create for ourselves and others by enabling us to eliminate violence, duplicity, animosity, and greed from our lives. Consequently, we are not a threat to others nor are others a threat to us. There is no ground for fear, and peace begins to grow.

Niyamas, the observances, also consists of five principles: purity, contentment, self-discipline, self-study, and surrender to God. These five principles open new channels for physical, mental, and spiritual nourishment. By purifying our thought, speech, and action we prepare ourselves to greet the Divine who resides within us. Contentment gives us freedom from anxiety, which otherwise is an enormous drain on our energy. Self-discipline frees us from laziness, giving us the opportunity to unfold our dormant potentials. Self-study allows us to identify our strengths and weaknesses. Self-study also includes the study of the scriptures and the repetition of mantras, observances which deepen our understanding of spirituality and improve our one-pointedness. These, in turn, motivate us to look for a higher purpose in life. Self-study frees us from attachment to our earlier, immature concepts of spirituality, enabling us to embrace an ever-expanding and ever more true reality. Surrender to God, the last of the observances, prevents us from becoming egotistical and helps us acknowledge and deepen our connection with the Divine. It is through surrender that divine grace flows into our lives.

These ten restraints and observances help us become simple, gentle, humble, disciplined, and kind—characteristics that are prerequisites to self-transformation. And by embracing them we prepare a solid foundation for whatever specific practice we undertake. Actually, these principles are themselves a complete path—simply by practicing them in their purity and perfection we can achieve freedom from the bondage of karma. But practicing even one to perfection requires a clear and one-pointed mind, an indomitable will, fearlessness, and a burning desire for liberation. And since we usually do not possess these characteristics and therefore cannot practice these principles with precision and perfection, the scriptures advise us to incorporate the yamas and niyamas into our philosophy of life and practice them to the best of our ability.

Practicing these restraints and observances in this mild fashion, however, does not guarantee that we will achieve freedom from the subtle traces of our karmas. As explained earlier, the subtle impressions stored in our unconscious mind are the direct cause of our personality traits. Powerful tendencies such as jealousy, greed, anger, and desire originate from the unconscious and are nourished by it; a passive practice is not powerful enough to neutralize them. That is why, for a deeper level of mental and behavioral cleansing, the *Yoga Sutra* and other scriptures prescribe the following fourfold practice:

Cultivate an attitude of friendship for those who are happy.
Cultivate compassion for those who are suffering.
Cultivate an attitude of cheerfulness toward those who seem to be virtuous.
Cultivate an attitude of indifference toward those who do not seem to be virtuous.

The ego is the root of all problems. It does not want to let go of its negative tendencies no matter how painful, degrading, or base they are because all tendencies and samskaras nourish the ego, and the ego delights in their presence. Negative tendencies—including anger, hatred, jealousy, greed, possessiveness, attachment, and desire—are part of the ego's wealth and it gets a sense of satisfaction from exhibiting this wealth, even though it becomes miserable in the process. Not knowing how to handle its self created misery, the ego searches for faults in others. This is true of all egos.

The most striking exhibition of ego is jealousy. Not only do we want to be happy and virtuous, we also want others to know that we're happy and virtuous. And further, we do not want anyone to be happier or more virtuous than we are. If we perceive that someone's happiness or virtue is greater than ours, the ego expresses itself in the form of animosity. Conversely, if someone appears to us to be more miserable or less virtuous than we are, the ego expresses itself by feeling superior.

These tendencies are a breeding ground for mental anguish, and as a result we lose our peace of mind. A person with a disturbed and confused mind cannot focus on the main goal of life. But letting go of our anger, jealousy, contempt, and animosity through cultivation of the four attitudes prescribed in the scriptures helps us compose our mind. And in the light of a composed and tranquil mind, we see things clearly. This is why the fourfold technique is known in yoga as *chitta prasadanam*—"mind purifier."

Yamaraja blessed Nachiketa by promising that his father would regain his peace of mind, lose his anger, and become cheerful. Further, the master promised that his father would become the way he used to be, that he would sleep well at night, and that when Nachiketa returned home he would acknowledge him. This blessing implies that any aspirant can attain the wisdom which will enable them to cultivate healthy interpersonal relationships and live a fulfilling life. In practical terms this blessing is acquired by cultivating the habit of letting go of anxieties and injuries, real or imagined. Forgetting and forgiving is the only way to sleep well at night. We must learn to communicate with each other in a loving, helpful, healthy way; we need to accept others the way they are and refrain from superimposing an image on them that we create in our own mind. Practicing the fourfold method of purifying the mind in conjunction with the ten restraints and observances enables us to do this. Thus we receive Nachiketa's first boon.

In addition, the first stage of spirituality also consists of specific and methodical practices that enable us to know ourselves at the level of body, breath, and mind. In the initial stages of our search, when we are neither strong in our convictions nor familiar with the unconscious contents of our mind, it is advisable to embrace a balanced path, one which combines elements of karma yoga (the yoga of selfless action), jnana yoga (the yoga of knowledge), bhakti yoga (the yoga of love and devotion), and hatha yoga. This balanced path is known as raja yoga, and the ten restraints and observances as well as the fourfold method of purifying the mind are an integral part it. Other components of raja yoga include physical exercises *(asana),* breathing techniques *(pranayama),* sense withdrawal *(pratyahara),* concentration *(dharana),* meditation *(dhyana),* and spiritual absorption *(samadhi).*

Regardless of differences in physical capacity, emotional maturity, and intellectual acuity, each of us can begin these practices at our own level. Raja yoga branches out into more specific paths, each leading directly to a specialized goal. And as we proceed we will gain a deeper insight into our own mind and body and thus automatically come to know which particular component of raja yoga should eventually be our main focus. For example, those who are interested in gaining a deeper understanding of their own body are attracted to hatha yoga; advanced practices of hatha yoga (consisting of *bandhas, mudras,* pranayama, visualization, and even alchemical practices) become their main path. Those interested in unveiling the mystery of the mind and unleashing its power find the concentration and meditation components of raja yoga most appealing. Those interested in knowing all—body, breath, mind, and soul, and their relationship with the Absolute—use hatha yoga and meditation as a stepping-stone to the practice of kundalini yoga.

Some of us are content to follow one of these paths, thinking that by so doing we are achieving the goal of life. After all, life does not seem to be troublesome anymore—no one is bothering us, we are not bothering anyone, and we are happier than we have ever been. We get into a routine and that routine itself becomes our spiritual practice.

But for others of us this is not enough. We find ourselves contemplating on the unpredictable nature of life and wondering what happens at the time of death. Where do we go after we die? We realize that no matter how healthy and well-balanced a life we are leading and no matter how virtuous that life is, one day it will be obliterated by death. These thoughts and questions cause us to become as concerned with dying gracefully as we are with living joyfully. We want to know the mystery of life after death. Does the soul really go to heaven or hell, and if so, does it continue its journey afterwards? Are there practices which can help us find answers to these questions? For those pondering these matters, the sages outline an entirely different set of practices, which form the intermediate stage of sadhana.

The Intermediate Stage

Our goals and objectives at this stage are well defined: we want to solve the mystery of life and death. The practices associated with the intermediate stage of the journey are advanced practices known as *vidyas* (spiritual sciences), and according to the scriptures they can be undertaken only by those who have a clear mind and know exactly what they are seeking. Further, this level of knowledge is reserved for those who cannot be influenced by any source outside themselves. The aspirant must have a firm intellectual grasp of the *vidyas* as well as firm faith in their master's knowledge and abilities. Those who feel the need to experiment with these sciences to test their validity are not fit for the practices. For example, it is only after understanding the dynamics of energy and matter contained in the formula $E = mc^2$ that a student of physics could even think of challenging Einstein. The same principle holds true for these spiritual sciences and the sages who discovered them.

This is demonstrated by Nachiketa's decisive statement in requesting the second boon from his master: "I have heard that in heaven there is no fear or old age. People are free from hunger and thirst. But only those who have transcended worries enjoy life there. I know you know the science of fire that unveils the mystery of heaven. I ask that you teach it to me, endowed as I am with faith."

Here Nachiketa is not asking whether or not heaven

exists—he knows; he is stating a fact. "Only those who have transcended worries enjoy life in heaven," he says, and this tells us that he is aware that attaining freedom from worries in this lifetime is a prerequisite to enjoying life in heaven after death. Nachiketa is not asking whether or not his master knows the science of fire. He is saying clearly that it is the science of fire that unveils the mystery of heaven and that his master is expert in that science. He is demonstrating that he has no doubt about the accuracy and depth of his master's knowledge. Further, his self-assurance is such that he can say, "I ask that you teach it to me, endowed as I am with faith." This reflects the perfect blend of humility and self-confidence that is a prerequisite for receiving this knowledge.

The science of fire that unveils the mystery of heaven is known in the yoga tradition as *agni vidya*. This is the ground where science and spirituality, yoga and mysticism, meet. The science is complex and is taught on two levels—*bahir yaga* (meditation on external fire) and *antar yaga* (meditation on internal fire)—but the practices pertaining to both are grounded in a common philosophy and metaphysics.

According to agni vidya, fire is both the origin and the intrinsic constituent of the universe. In other words, the universe is fire in another form. Fire is both the force of transformation and the object being transformed. Matter and energy are both aspects of fire. Fire exists in two forms: ignited, and unignited. In the scriptures these are referred to in terms of awakened and dormant energy; awakened fire has the capacity to ignite the fire that lies dormant. Agni vidya further holds that it is only out of ignorance that we see fire solely in its physical aspects: fire is an intelligent entity; it is fire's intelligence that makes us intelligent. When fire withdraws itself, its intelligence withdraws and we become lifeless, inert.

We have become so materialistically minded that we do not have an accurate perspective concerning the reality of fire. In our daily life we see fire simply as a resource or commodity. It never occurs to us that fire is an intelligent force with inherent consciousness. Our obtuseness has created a barrier that prevents us from communicating with—and communing with—the spirit of fire. Yet the scriptures tell us that it is possible to overcome this barrier and to receive guidance directly from the fire. The way to communicate with fire is in the language of mantras—agni vidya (the science of fire) and mantra vidya (the science of mantras) are complementary. Through the power of mantra we awaken the external fire, and this awakened fire in turn awakens the dormant fire within us.

The sages laid out a complex and methodical way of awakening fire both externally and internally. Just as Yamaraja explained to Nachiketa how fire is the primordial principle and the source of the universe, the adepts who have mastered this science (who in our modern times are very rare, and even more rarely encountered) give practical lessons on how to invoke the fire as an intelligent force residing in non-intelligent matter. They explain how to ignite it and place it in the *kunda,* the ceremonial firepit, and, further, tell us how to build the firepit. Before fusing two atoms, scientists prepare the lab, assemble the proper containers, and create conditions for capturing the energy released by the fusion. So do the masters of agni vidya prepare the appropriate kind of ceremonial firepit. The selection of its site, its size and shape, as well as the number of bricks used in building it, all follow scientific rules and laws codified in the scriptures.

The presence of the pranic force gives life to our body. In

the same way, the power of mantra gives life to the firepit, transforming it into a living entity. There are *marmasthanas* (centers of vital energy) and chakras (centers of consciousness) in our body, which we can identify. The adepts of agni vidya teach the aspirant where the *marma* points and chakras are located in the firepit.

The science of fire taught by Yamaraja to Nachiketa explains how, by meditating on external fire with rituals and mantra recitation, we can identify the centers of vital energy in the firepit, penetrate them by performing a threefold ritual, and use the energy generated by this ritual to cross the river of birth and death. But this technique can give the impression that agni vidya is merely a religious ritual—an impression which has substance only if we are not familiar with Vedic metaphysics, in which agni vidya and mantra vidya are central themes. Therefore the yogic sages, realizing that this aspect of agni vidya could create religious conflicts in many people's minds, have always advised aspirants to learn how to invoke the internal fire, a practice that does not involve ritual.

Meditation on the internal fire requires that an aspirant learn the techniques for activating the energies which lie dormant at the navel center. This is the *manipura* chakra—"the chakra filled with gems"; it is also known as *mani padma*—"the lotus made of shining gems." Ordinarily our mind is occupied with the issues of the two lowest chakras: the *muladhara* (the center at the base of the spine) and the *svadhishthana* (the pelvic center). Because these two chakras are the seat of the four primitive urges [hunger, sleep, sex, and self-preservation], they govern issues related to fear, hunger, survival, sensual pleasure, desire, and attachment. They diminish the fire at the third chakra, the navel center, and block our access to it.

According to mystical literature the third chakra corresponds to the heavenly realm within. It is the center of the vibrant energy which nourishes the whole body and mind; the healing force resides here; it is the seat of enthusiasm, courage, self-motivation, and indomitable will.

The fire at the navel center is the source of our existence. The fetus is connected to the mother through this center. Although desire for progeny flashes in the mind and manifests in the form of the biological urge at the second chakra, the life-force which desires to manifest lies at the navel center. In fact, it is the outward movement of the life-force at the navel center that motivates the mind to desire progeny and activates the second chakra. Thus the process of our outward journey—birth—begins at the navel center. By the same token, the mystery that lies behind the curtain of birth can be unveiled at the navel center. The *Katha Upanishad* (1:1:18) clearly states, "After knowing the science of fire a learned seeker who gathers this Nachiketa agni cuts asunder the snares of death, transcends all worries, and enjoys life in heaven."

Before we can experience the illumination and nourishment inherent in the navel center, however, we must ignite the fire, and this requires rising above the issues of the first two chakras. But once we are fully established in the first stage of practice, we can turn our mind inward and commit ourselves to the higher practices.

According to the *Svetashvatara Upanishad* (2:6), "The mind is drawn to the center where fire is being churned, prana is being retained, or the energies of soma [the sensual energies] are heavily concentrated." This means that in order to introduce our mind to the third chakra we must either churn the fire at the navel center, or practice breath retention, or pull the sensual energies up from the first and second chakras and concentrate them at the third chakra. By applying any or all of these methods we illuminate the mind, bringing it out of the darkness of the first two chakras. And those who have penetrated *rudra granthi* (the knot at the navel center) are blessed with the light of the fire of the manipura chakra.

Agni vidya, or mastery over the navel center, unveils many other mysteries. As the *Yoga Sutra* states, "By practicing special techniques of meditation at the navel center, yogis gain complete knowledge of their bodies" (3:29). Further, "Meditation at the solar plexus enables yogis to understand the entire dynamics of the celestial realm—the sun, moon, stars, planets, and the galaxies which rotate around the polar star" (3:26). Yogis unveiling this mystery can perceive and communicate with the beings who reside in the celestial realm without having material bodies. The joy derived from this extraordinary knowledge and experience supersedes our sensory pleasure; therefore, in a sense it is heavenly joy. It is in that sense that the scriptures say that through agni vidya yogis gather the inner fire, transcend worries, and enjoy life in heaven. The *Yoga Sutra* calls these yogic achievements *siddhis*.

The aspect of agni vidya that involves meditation on the internal fire includes the higher techniques of hatha yoga, kundalini yoga, and mantra yoga. A perfect blend of these techniques is often described in highly acclaimed tantric scriptures—such as *Rudra Yamala* and *Svachchhanda Tantra*—as well as in the *Katha, Svetashvatara,* and *Dhyanabindu* Upanishads. The greatest repository of these techniques, however, are the texts belonging to the yogis of the Natha tradition.

Gaining extraordinary knowledge and experience is very exciting, but if we are not diligent in pursuing the highest purpose of life it can become an obstacle in our spiritual journey by distracting us from our goal and feeding our ego. Regardless of how much knowledge we gain on the path and how many mysteries we have unveiled, if it does not lead to complete freedom from the cycle of birth and death it is of little value. In the Bhagavad Gita (9:21) Krishna says, "Having enjoyed the celestial pleasures, when their virtues [gained through yogic practices and meritorious deeds] are exhausted, people return to this mortal world again. Thus those who, intent on receiving rewards, undertake practices described in the scriptures remain caught in the cycle of birth and death."

Thus we see that through the practice of agni vidya we can illuminate our thoughts and emotions, live a heavenly life on this plane, and continue to enjoy heavenly pleasures after death. This does not mean, however, that we have attained complete freedom from the cycle of birth and death. Far from it. Agni vidya simply gives us access to the navel center "filled with gems," and with this access we no longer suffer from the poverty of mind imposed upon us when we dwell in the first two chakras. The knowledge of heaven and hell—the bright and dark avenues of our unconscious—appears to be a great achievement only to those who lack a higher purpose in life. For no matter how well we know the mysteries of heaven and hell, we cannot attain freedom until we transcend them and reach the realm beyond. According to the scriptures, if we neglect the higher purpose of life, sooner or later we exhaust our store of gems and find ourselves back in the realm dominated by worry, anxiety, and fear. That is why a sincere aspirant like Nachiketa does not become complacent. He is not satisfied with this level of knowledge alone. This realization pushes us to the third and final stage of sadhana.

The joy a master finds in meeting a fully prepared student like Nachiketa is evident when Yamaraja teaches him the science of agni vidya. When Nachiketa demonstrates that he has mastered it, Yamaraja is so pleased that he pours out another blessing. Through this blessing the master clears the path so that one day Nachiketa will master even higher aspects of yoga science.

The Final Stage of Sadhana

After Nachiketa had mastered agni vidya and its related yogic sciences, he realized he was still wandering in the transitory world, essentially no different from a migratory bird. He therefore asked for the knowledge that could lead him beyond this realm. In response to the temptations Yamaraja offered in place of this boon, Nachiketa said, "Worldly objects are short-lived. They may or may not last until tomorrow. They consume the life of our senses. No matter how long we live, it is not enough. Therefore, O Gurudeva, please keep your chariots, elephants, and dancing girls for yourself.

"A human being can never be satiated with wealth. After seeing you, Gurudeva, I know that if I need wealth, I will get it; and I know that I will continue to live as long as you wish. Therefore, I insist on the boon that I have requested. After meeting an immortal sage like you, how can a mortal person still long for short-lived worldly pleasures and a long life?"

In other words, even though Nachiketa had gained knowledge of the earthly and celestial realms, it only fed his longing to know the eternal truth and his relationship with it. This is the criterion for graduating from the intermediate to the final stage of sadhana: this stage is for those rare seekers whose every desire, including the desire for heaven, is consumed by the desire for knowing the truth which is eternal, self-illumined, and divine. This is the highest form of *vairagya* (nonattachment), and it is the prerequisite to both *nirbija* (seedless) samadhi and *parabhakti* (the highest form of devotion to God). At the dawning of this level of nonattachment, the fire of true knowledge ignites by itself and consumes all the subtle impressions of our past. The charms and temptations of this world and the celestial realm no longer attract us, because our heart is somewhere else. Our longing to taste the immortal nectar is so strong that worldly and celestial pleasures become tasteless.

At this stage, those seekers who have a strong orientation toward knowledge long only for self-realization, and this by its very nature involves experiencing our oneness with the Absolute. Those, on the other hand, with a strong orientation toward *bhakti*—love and devotion—long to have a direct experience of the Divine, and when they do, they merge with the Beloved.

Whichever form it takes, this final stage of the spiritual journey transcends all mundane and heavenly achievements. Aspirants who have been endowed with both deep knowledge and strong *bhakti* from the earliest stages of the journey prefer to bypass the second stage by following the path of contemplation, meditation, or prayer and absorbing their mind in the Divine Being. With the help of knowledge and nonattachment they burn all their samskaras, and through their unwavering faith and their love for the Divine their entire unconscious is filled with divine awareness. Whether they leave their body in a yogic manner or die in an ordinary fashion, these yogis go to the realm that transcends the cycle of birth and death, heaven and hell.

In the Bhagavad Gita, Lord Krishna stresses the importance of cultivating such a high level of purity and one-pointedness of mind that at the time of death the mind fixes exclusively on the Lord of Life who resides within us. Only then do we enter the realm beyond, which shines through its own effulgence. In Krishna's words, "One who at the time of death remembers me alone becomes one with my essence. There is no doubt about it" (Bhagavad Gita 8:5). He then goes on to say, "Those who are fully established in yoga with an unwavering mind leave their bodies contemplating only on the Divine Being and thus reach the realm of the Divine. . . . With a stable mind, those endowed with the power of yoga and *j*—who make their entire pranic force enter the center between the eyebrows and thus leave the body—reach the realm beyond. . . . Controlling all the gates, confining the mind in the heart, placing the pranic force in the crown of the head, thus fully established in yoga, one who, remembering me alone, leaves the body with the sound of "Om" goes to the supreme realm." (Bhagavad Gita 8:8,10,12–13)

Often in our ignorance we think we can wait until our old age to commit ourselves to spirituality, believing that the subtle impressions created by spiritual practices will come forward at the time of death and enable us to attain freedom from transmigration. We forget that in the past countless numbers of people have made similar plans, but failed to materialize them. We do not realize that the desires, attachments, and forces of the unconscious mind which today are actively advising us to postpone making an unwavering commitment to our practice will become even more active as we age—and that as we grow old, our impatience also grows, the senses become weak, retentive power declines, and hopelessness dominates our entire being. In such a state of body and mind, how can we faithfully commit ourselves to an intense, prolonged practice? And if indeed we are to form and accumulate spiritually illuminating samskaras of knowledge, love, and devotion, then we need to practice faithfully for a long period of time without interruption—so we need to begin as soon as possible.

That is why the scriptures advise us to begin our spiritual quest right here and right now, before it's too late. To pacify ourselves we say that it's never too late, but the truth is that for one who is ignorant it is never too late, while for one who is wise it is never too early. The journey toward death begins at the moment of birth. The sooner we start the spiritual journey the better.

The good news is that we are always surrounded by the grace of the Divine, and in spite of the law of karma and the forces of destiny, all of us are guided and protected by this grace. No matter how good or bad we are, how sincere or insincere, the Divine dwells always in our heart. It takes only a moment to realize that this internal friend is always with us, and when we fully realize that truth, we are suffused with an overwhelming sense of oneness with the Divine. From this moment on, no force in the world can hinder our journey. That is why the sages tell us, "Be not disheartened, O child of Divinity. The light you are seeking burns within you. Surrender and it will unveil itself to you." Thus for one who treads the path of love and divine ecstasy, it is never too late. The destination rushes toward the seeker.

ABOUT THE AUTHOR

As Spiritual Head of the Himalayan International Institute, Pandit Rajmani Tigunait, Ph.D., is the successor of Swami Rama of the Himalayas. A lifelong practitioner of meditation and a Sanskrit scholar, he has studied with various adepts and scholars in the time-honored guru/disciple lineage. He holds a doctorate in Sanskrit from the University of Allahabad in India, and a doctorate in philosophy from the University of Pennsylvania. In addition to having written ten books, Pandit Tigunait lectures throughout the world and is a regular contributor to *Yoga International* magazine.

The main building of the Institute headquarters
near Honesdale, Pennsylvania

THE HIMALAYAN INSTITUTE

FOUNDED IN 1971 BY SWAMI RAMA, the Himalayan
Institute has been dedicated to helping people grow physically,
mentally, and spiritually by combining the best knowledge of
both the East and the West.

Our international headquarters is located on a beautiful 400-
acre campus in the rolling hills of the Pocono Mountains of
northeastern Pennsylvania. The atmosphere here is one to foster
growth, increased inner awareness, and calm. Our grounds
provide a wonderfully peaceful and healthy setting for our
seminars and extended programs. Students from around the
world join us here to attend programs in such diverse areas as
hatha yoga, meditation, stress reduction, Ayurveda, nutrition,
Eastern philosophy, psychology, and other subjects. Whether the

programs are for weekend meditation retreats, week-long seminars on spirituality, months-long residential programs, or holistic health services, the attempt here is to provide an environment of gentle inner progress. We invite you to join with us in the ongoing process of personal growth and development. The Institute is a nonprofit organization. Your membership in the Institute helps to support its programs. Please call or write for information on becoming a member.

INSTITUTE PROGRAMS, SERVICES, AND FACILITIES

Institute programs share an emphasis on conscious holistic living and personal self-development, including:

Special weekend or extended seminars to teach skills and techniques for increasing your ability to be healthy and enjoy life

Meditation retreats and advanced meditation and philosophical instruction

Vegetarian cooking and nutritional training

Hatha yoga and exercise workshops

Residential programs for self-development

Holistic health services and Ayurvedic Rejuvenation Programs through the Institute's Center for Health and Healing.

A *Quarterly Guide to Programs and Other Offerings* is free within the USA. To request a copy, or for further information, call 800-822-4547 or 570-253-5551, fax 570-253-9078, email bqinfo@himalayaninstitute.org, write the Himalayan Institute, RR 1 Box 400, Honesdale, PA 18431-9706 USA or visit our website at www.himalayaninstitute.org.

THE HIMALAYAN INSTITUTE PRESS

THE HIMALAYAN INSTITUTE PRESS has long been regarded as "The Resource for Holistic Living." We publish dozens of titles, as well as audio and video tapes, that offer practical methods for living harmoniously and achieving inner balance. Our approach addresses the whole person—body, mind, and spirit—integrating the latest scientific knowledge with ancient healing and self-development techniques.

As such, we offer a wide array of titles on physical and psychological health and well-being, spiritual growth through meditation and other yogic practices, as well as translations of yogic scriptures.

Our sidelines include the Japa Kit for meditation practice, the Neti™ Pot, the ideal tool for sinus and allergy sufferers, and The Breath Pillow,™ a unique tool for learning health-supportive diaphragmatic breathing.

Subscriptions are available to a bimonthly magazine, *Yoga International,* which offers thought-provoking articles on all aspects of meditation and yoga, including yoga's sister science, Ayurveda.

For a free catalog call 800-822-4547 or 570-253-5551, email hibooks@himalayaninstitute.org, fax 570-253-6360, write the Himalayan Institute Press, RR 1, Box 405, Honesdale, PA 18431-9709, USA, or visit our Web site at www.himalayaninstitute.org.